Tales of Old N

Tales of Old Northamptonshire

Marian Pipe

With Illustrations by Don Osmond

COUNTRYSIDE BOOKS
NEWBURY, BERKSHIRE

First Published 1990
© Marian Pipe 1990
Reprinted 1991, 1993

COUNTRYSIDE BOOKS
3 CATHERINE ROAD
NEWBURY, BERKSHIRE

ISBN 1 85306 087 9

Produced through MRM Associates Ltd., Reading
Printed in England

To my husband
David Edward Pipe

Contents

CONTENTS

NORTHAMPTONSHIRE – The map overleaf is by John Speede and shows the county as it was in the early seventeenth century.

The
Hollywood of
Northamptonshire

IRTHLINGBOROUGH is a small town bypassed by the A6 road, which is taken over the river Nene by a massive viaduct and looks down on the 15th century stone bridge. In the long high street stands the old Horseshoe inn. Today it is a popular but modest establishment, and it is difficult to imagine that in the early years of the 20th century it was the headquarters of a film company. The little town of Irthlingborough became, for a while, the centre of the silent movie industry in Great Britain.

Charles Weston was an American from Jacksonville, producing films for a company called The British and Colonial Kinematograph. This firm was renowned in England for using more daring and original scripts than their rivals. They even took their cameramen and actors on location, which was then almost unheard of, instead of relying on a studio in the city.

Weston came to the district in search of a location for a new film about Napoleon and the Duke of

11

Wellington. Perhaps someone had told him that the Iron Duke had once said that the countryside between Woodford and Irthlingborough was similar to the land on which the battle of Waterloo had been fought. He stayed the night at the Horseshoe and decided to make the spectacular film *The Battle of Waterloo* in the area.

Joe Inward was the tenant landlord of the pub at the time, and the town's fire officer. His daughter Alice was to become Weston's wife. Alice's brother Jack was given a small part in the film as aide-de-camp to the Duke of Wellington. Charles Weston and the film industry made a great impact on the ordinary, respectable Inward family. Their lives were suddenly turned upside down by this thrilling event. The family moved into a farmhouse in College Street, a short distance from the pub, and the film company used the Horseshoe as their headquarters.

One Monday morning in June, 1913, the filming began. A large crowd gathered outside the Horseshoe as early as 5 am to watch developments, but not much happened before eight o'clock. Irthlingborough that summer morning was already a hive of noise and bustle, when a hundred men of the 12th Lancers from Weedon Barracks rode into town to take part in the film. They were billeted at the old skating rink. Men from the workhouse, and other unemployed people from Northampton, were brought in to take part as extras. It was no small undertaking to try and fit 500–600 men with uniforms as French, Prussian and English troops, on that June morning. A good part of the day had gone before proceedings began.

The sleepy little town of Irthlingborough, with its population of barely 5,000, had never seen anything like it. The event caused such excitement that many people stayed off from work to watch. In fact the shoe factories of Lilley and Shortland had shut on the Monday morning, anticipating the absence of a lot of their operators.

Jack Inward had been given the task of scouring the neighbourhood for as many old cabs and wagons as he could get his hands on, so that the axles could be used for mounting the guns. The main characters in the film were brought down from London, the part of Napoleon being played by Ernest G. Batley. The battle scenes were made more realistic by bringing dead horses in from the knacker's yard at Rushden and spreading them around the field.

On Tuesday morning the shoe factories opened, but in the afternoon many of the workers failed to turn up. The firms of Lilley and Shortland decided to take the high-handed step of closing down for the rest of the week. As an article in the *Kettering Leader* dated Friday the 13th June, 1913, pointed out: 'This means a thousand men and women of the working class will have no wages this week. It seems unjust that those who were loyal to the firms they served should be thrown out of work for so many days, because of the disloyalty of the others.'

It was some consolation to some of the inhabitants that they were able to earn seven shillings and sixpence per day as extras in the film, whereas normally their wages were only 30 shillings a week in a shoe factory.

Thousands of people poured into Irthlingborough

to watch the motion picture being made, especially on Tuesday afternoon when the battle scenes were being shot. These took place on land behind Three Chimnies, on the sloping ground of Feast Field and on a large flat field belonging to Mr Wilkins on the Findon road. It was on this field that many of the spectators were to be found, standing three or four deep around the edge, some of them even climbing up the trees for a better view. The crowd were in a good humour. They were amused to see Charles Weston, who was wearing riding breeches and a check cap, giving instructions to Napoleon and Wellington with the aid of a massive megaphone. He shouted to some of the soldiers fighting at close quarters 'that when he told them to die, then they should die.' For the men were enjoying the novelty of acting so much they were forgetting to lie down. The horses also had their parts to play. Often they wouldn't go past the camera fast enough, so one of the soldiers left his post and with a little encouragement from a long stick, urged them to move a little quicker.

The town had a marvellous week of film making and the pubs were drunk dry. Sadly, many of the men who were taking part in the film battle would be fighting in a real war a year later in 1914.

It was by no means the only film to be made in Irthlingborough. There was *The Life of Queen Victoria* and *The Seventh Day* which made great use of the Horseshoe inn as a setting. Another picture *Through the Clouds*, attracted a lot of attention. It was an adventure story, making use of balloons and aeroplanes. However, the film which really made the best use of local talent was called *The Poacher's Sweetheart*. It was a melodramatic tale of love at the Manor, missing marriage lines and a dastardly plot to implicate the hero for a murder he didn't commit. It was written by a local author, Cliff Warren, and many of the town's residents had acting parts. The main characters were played by the Inward family. Jack played the poacher, his wife played Eva the heroine. Jack's mother, Betty, had a small part, and even the six year old grandson Joseph Spring had a part as a messenger boy.

At least one more film was made at Irthlingborough, entitled *Called to the Front*. It had a showing in Canada, Britain and on the Continent. Despite its lavish battle scenes, it was rather a boring film. The British Kinematograph Company went into decline, but Charles Weston and Arthur Finn went on to found a company called Regent Films, which had a studio in Queen's Road in Bayswater.

Irthlingborough settled back to being a small, ordinary town again, and the Inward family reverted to living their quiet lives. Except for Alice, who went to live with her husband Charles Weston in the USA. The Horseshoe inn was once more a typical English pub, but the talk of the locals for years was of the exciting time when Irthlingborough nearly became an international film centre. Or, who knows, another Hollywood!

The
Great Fire of
Wellingborough

THE bustling town of Wellingborough has
expanded greatly over the last few decades, but it
has still managed to retain a few old buildings of
historical interest. All Hallows, the parish church, is
one of them. It has a 13th century tower and spire, six
remarkable misericords, and superb modern stained
glass windows. The church stands next to the market
square, and facing the churchyard is the ancient
grammar school, now the church hall. It was founded
in 1595, with its two adjoining houses of the same
period.

Wellingborough is fortunate also to possess two old
inns in the middle of the town, the picturesque 16th
century Golden Lion and the imposing Hind Hotel in
Sheep Street, whilst close by is the fine 15th century
tithe barn of thatch and iron-stone, which is well-used
for various public activities.

Like many old towns, Wellingborough has had its
share of fires in the past, and one of them in the 18th

century nearly destroyed its fine old buildings. An informative pamphlet in All Hallows' church, written by Canon Methuen Clarke in 1949, describes how an entry in the parish register recalls that fateful day. 'On July 28th 1738 happened a terrible fire at 2 of the clock in the afternoon and in less than four hours consumed the best part of the town, it was a Fryday.'

It had been a wonderful summer that year, with no rain falling for weeks. The tiny thatched cottages with tinder-dry roofs, huddled closely together. A local industry on the west side of the town was cloth dyeing. In a yard behind one of these dyers' shops, in Silver Street, a boy was drying oats. The warmth of the sun and the heat from the kiln made him dozy, and before he realized what had happened a spark from the fire had flown onto the barn of a neighbour. It immediately caught fire and began to spread to other buildings.

The south-west wind fanned the flames in a slanting direction to the butchery. It was here that one house was saved in a remarkable way. When the water supply failed, Mrs Hannah Sparke (an appropriate name) ordered her servants to go down to the cellar and draw out all the beer. Resourceful Hannah, who was 60 years old at the time, told them to soak all the blankets in beer that they could lay their hands on, and to spread them over the roof of her home. This action stopped the thatch from catching alight.

Though the Sparke residence had been saved, the all-consuming fire continued on its way. It burned down the buildings in Pebble Lane, and swept across to Market Street, Cambridge Street and Cannon Street

17

destroying most of the buildings in its way. Terrified men, women and children fled before it, having no time to rescue their possessions. Many of them sought refuge in the parish church, where the intense heat of the fire melted the lead on the roof, which flowed into the gutters and onto the ground. Fortunately the damage to the church stopped there.

The pathetic equipment of the fire fighters consisted of buckets and staves, and was completely inadequate. The heat of the inferno drove them back. An urgent appeal to the neighbouring town of Kettering was sent, where the thick pall of smoke from the great fire of Wellingborough could be seen eight miles away. They helped by sending their primitive fire engine, pulled by horses that struggled and sweated over the rolling countryside between the two towns.

A desperate measure was finally taken by the people of the town when they set alight a field of corn, which acted as a fire break and brought the inferno under control. Then the citizens of Wellingborough took stock of their town. It had been a disastrous fire. They found that miraculously no lives had been lost, but 600 people were homeless and 200 houses had been burned down, as well as hundreds of barns, shops, outhouses and stables.

Help came from many sources to rebuild the town. The people of Northampton sent 300 guineas, 100 guineas came from Kettering and 40 guineas from Oundle. Monies also came from the gentry, making up a grand total of 560 guineas.

Although that was the end of the fire, it was not the

last that Wellingborough heard of Hannah Sparke, for this indomitable old lady, born in October 1678, lived to see her century and more. At the grand old age of 100, Hannah was ceremoniously chaired around the square where she lived by her friends and neighbours, in an atmosphere of triumph and rejoicing. Old Hannah died on the 11th September 1785, aged 107.

A curious postscript for this tale comes from an article in the *Kettering Advertiser* dated Friday the 24th of November, 1911. It would seem that the exact whereabouts of this grand old lady's last resting place had been forgotten. That year contractors, Messrs Hacksley Bros, were putting in a new heating system in All Hallows' Church. It was necessary to excavate below the Lady chapel, on the south side and near to the main entrance. When they laid the hot air tracks a portion of the central aisle of the church was taken up, and there near to the font they come across the grave of Hannah Sparke. There was an inscription on the lid of the leaden coffin in raised letters, which stated very clearly the name of Hannah Sparke and her age of 107. The casket was only 18 inches below the stone slab and was five feet in length, and it rested on an empty lead coffin. It was decided to move the coffin about two feet nearer to the east end and cover it over. A brief mention is made of this famous centenarian on the walls of the parish church of All Hallows.

The
Martyr of
Lois Weedon

IN a maze of lanes and byways between the two towns
of Brackley and Towcester lies the quiet village of
Lois Weedon, as the locals like to call it, but which is
marked on modern maps and signs as Weedon Lois.

The parish church dedicated to St Mary and St Peter
is partly Norman and has a central low tower with
embattlements. In the churchyard the gravestones
stand upright upon the well mown turf. A border of
delphiniums and pink roses lines the pathway to the
church.

Inside, a brass tablet on the wall, erected by public
subscription in 1899, tells of thrilling events which
once took place here. 'William Losse of King's College,
Cambridge, for 25 years vicar of Lois Weedon. He was
a faithful churchman and affectionate husband and
father. On his refusal to surrender his person and
living to a detachment of twelve soldiers, he was fired
upon with pistols many times within this church, was
finally pierced with swords and in a baptism of blood

was left for dead upon the roof of the tower, Sunday 2nd July 1643. He was one of 7,000 clergymen who, for the honour of God, and for the witness of his truth as expressed in the tenets of the Church of England were contented (in those evil and cruel times) to suffer murder, violence and insult, to be dragged from their benefices, and cast with their families upon the world, forbidden to earn their bread as scholars, or else sent to die upon the hulks, or in prison, or in foreign slavery. Of whom at the Restoration only 600 survived to resume their livings.'

It is peaceful in the church, the only sound the singing of the birds outside and the church clock striking. The past seems very far away. It is almost impossible to imagine that violence and murder took place in this holy spot, over 300 years ago.

It was in 1642 that the Civil War in England had begun. The residents of Northampton were sympathetic to the Parliamentarian cause and early in 1641, as the signs of conflict between King Charles I and Parliament increased, the Corporation of Northampton had begun to prepare against a possible attack on the town. They gave orders to take stones from a ruined church and repair the broken-down walls of Northampton and strengthen and mend the gates. The town was to become one of the strongest garrisons of the Parliamentarian army in the South Midlands.

In the turbulent times of the Civil War the inhabitants of the small village of Lois Weedon went quietly on with their own lives. William Losse, their vicar of long standing, was respected and admired by

22

the villagers. He had been in the community since 1618, when the living had been presented to him by the provost and scholars of King's College, Cambridge, which held the tithes and advowson of Lois Weedon.

The fact that Rev Losse had been ministering to his flock for so long does not seem to have impressed the Roundhead officials at Northampton. For Rev Losse was a zealous Royalist and his beliefs had greatly offended the local Puritans.

William Losse lived in the vicarage next to the church with his wife Elizabeth and their six children. In 1643 on that fateful Sunday, twelve Roundhead troopers burst into the church with the intention of taking the clergyman back to Northampton as their prisoner. They advanced towards the reading desk where he was conducting the service. The leader stepped forward and commanded the vicar to 'leave off his pottage,' and follow him. William asked to be allowed to finish his devotions, but they refused.

Rev Losse followed them into the churchyard, where he was told that he must accompany them back to the town immediately. The outraged vicar asked them to explain on whose authority they had been sent. But the only answer they gave was that he would find out soon enough on his arrival. Rev Losse stated that he had already been robbed of his horses by the Parliamentarian soldiers, and he hadn't one left. One of the troopers told him he could ride behind him, or he would be dragged along with a halter at his horse's tail. The vicar was roused by the man's impudence, and replied forthrightly that 'he would never be a slave to slaves.'

The soldiers were to discover that this was no cowardly cleric, who would give into their demands without a struggle. For William broke away from them and took refuge in the church, barring the door behind him. The congregation by now were trying to leave by the opposite door, but they were being impeded by one of the soldiers trying to ride his horse into the church. Rev Losse dashed over and attacked the insolent trooper with the door bar, and tried to knock him off his horse. 'Which made the fellow keep off, and so Rev Losse got time to bar the door likewise.'

The other door was now being hammered on, and William made his escape to the tower. He reached the leads by a trapdoor, and managed to drag the ladder up behind him and laid it across the opening. The soldiers by now had broken into the church, using pole axes and tombstones from the churchyard to batter down the door, and rode into the building. 'Spurring and switching their horses, purposely to endanger the people.' Some of the congregation were still inside the church, and a few of them even dared to speak up for their vicar, imploring the soldiers to leave him alone. They reminded the Roundheads that, 'Rev Losse was a gentleman of a good family.' The officer in charge of the men would not listen to their pleas and sneered 'What do you tell me of birth and descent? A plague take him and his gentility. I hope within this year to see never a gentleman in England.'

Whereupon they charged into the tower and up to the trapdoor. The soldiers fired their pistols through the entrance, eight or nine times, but did not manage to shoot the valiant vicar. Next they thrust their swords

24

through the opening and Rev Losse was wounded in several places. His blood flowed in a fast stream down upon the attackers beneath him. It was then that the troopers concluded that their mission had been accomplished, and bragged about the deed, saying that 'they thought they had dispatched him.'

Subsequent events are unfortunately vague, and whether Rev Losse died that morning or some time later can never be proved, for the parish registers between 1637 and 1698 are missing.

The vicar's family seems to have had a harrowing time even after the death of the Rev Losse, for in 1644 his son was accused of 'bringing enemy spoils home to the house of his mother.' But perhaps the family were allowed to live in peace after 1645, when William Losse's will was proved by his wife, on the 23rd of August of that year.

The Pioneer Missionary

WILLIAM Carey the pioneer missionary, has been acclaimed by many people as this county's greatest son. He was born in the village of Paulerspury on the 17th of March, 1761, where his father had been the village schoolmaster for an amazing 50 years. The family of Carey had been connected with Paulerspury for many years, for William's grandfather had also taken up the duties of parish clerk and school teacher.

William was the eldest son of a family of five children. His father had been a weaver, like his father before him, before he was offered the post of schoolmaster. Even so the family were very poor. William's keen intelligence and aptitude for learning showed up at a very early age. He was a normal happy-go-lucky type of boy, with a boy's love of the open air. As the oldest son he was given a tiny room to himself, which he filled with as many books as he could get his hands on and crammed with insects and live birds in every corner. He loved to read books on science, history and travel, but disliked novels. The young scholar was earnest in all his pursuits, recreational as well as scholastic. As he walked the country lanes, he carefully studied and observed everything he saw about him. The thick woods of

Whittlebury forest, which lay near to his home were one of his favourite haunts. At the age of twelve William discovered his remarkable gift for languages, and taught himself Latin from a book called *Dyche's Latin Vocabulary*.

His father soon realized that William was not fit enough to work in the fields, because of a painful skin disease, so he had him apprenticed into the boot and shoe trade at the age of 14. Clever as his son was, he couldn't afford to let him carry on with his studies any longer. His first employer was Charles Nichols, a quick-tempered shoemaker at Hackleton, a village nine miles from Paulerspury.

Mr Nichols died after William had only worked for him a year. He was then transferred to Mr Old, also of Hackleton. A fellow apprentice persuaded Carey to attend a dissenters' meeting in the same village, and he was converted in 1779. William worked at Hackleton but lived in Piddington close by, and as many evenings as he could spare, he would pore over the voyages of Captain Cook, enthralled by what he read. Whilst at this village he met the Rev Thomas Scott, who was a famous Bible commentator. Rev Scott helped William to study the scriptures, and called the little cobbler's shop at Hackleton, 'Carey's College'. He also recognised Carey's outstanding qualities and predicted that he was destined for great things.

Another milestone in William's life came in 1783, when he walked the six miles to Northampton and was baptised in the river Nene below the castle, by John Ryland of College Lane chapel. Carey had first appeared in the pulpit at the age of 19. He was a natural preacher and for the next three and a half years he went around the villages of Earls Barton and Hackleton preaching the gospel.

On the 10th of July 1781 William married Dorothy Plackett in the church at Piddington. Dorothy was the sister-in-law of Mr Old, she was illiterate and five years older than Carey. William and his wife went to live at Moulton, for he had heard that there was a need for a school teacher in the village. He was also obliged to do cobbling to supplement his meagre earnings.

The Baptists at Moulton had been without a minister for some years and their church was neglected and delapidated, so they asked Carey if he would be their pastor. He soon increased his congregation with his fervour, and improved the building by appealing to his friends for £100 to reconstruct and enlarge the chapel. His terraced cottage had only one room up and one room down, and was but a few doors away from his church.

At his little school, which was probably in the small workshop at the rear of the cottage, he taught a few boys to read and write. Poverty prevented him from providing the pupils with any tools and he had only a few books. But William industriously sewed a few pieces of leather to make a globe, on which he painted the continents and seas. He wanted to arouse their curiosity about lands beyond their own. He also drew a large map of the world on the wall of his home. Over a period of years he collected as many facts and figures as he could about the peoples of the world, their religions, occupations and populations. The result of all this research was later published as *The Enquiry*.

This detailed and scientific book set out his theories and arguments of the need for a world-wide mission of the church. It was published in 1792.

As though it wasn't enough to be pastor, cobbler and teacher, William still found time to learn four languages – Dutch, Hebrew, Greek and French. He was ordained as a minister on the 10th of August, 1786.

Not all his fellow Baptists shared Carey's enthusiasm for spreading their faith in foreign lands. At a meeting of Baptist ministers in 1788, at Northampton, Carey was told sharply to sit down when he tried to speak of his cherished beliefs in the cause. Over the next twelve years, Carey planned and strove to attain his dream of becoming a missionary.

William and his family moved from Moulton to Leicester where he took up a new ministry. His ideas on foreign missionary work eventually aroused the interest of a small group of Baptist pastors in Kettering. On the 2nd of October, 1792 an historic meeting took place in the home of Widow Beeby Wallis. A group of young Baptist ministers sat in the small back parlour of the house, and the Particular Baptist Society was formed, now known as the Baptist Missionary Society. At last William was on his way to be a missionary. Nearly a year later, Carey, his wife and four children, disembarked at Calcutta, on the 11th November 1793, as the Society's first missionary.

Carey already had a heavy burden to bear when he arrived in India, for his wife Dorothy was mentally ill and was to get steadily worse. His party were soon in financial difficulties, and Carey had to take up his old trade of cobbling to support his family. The missionary built a bamboo house in the jungle, on a few acres of land which was rent free for three years. What a strange and frightening place it must have been for his sick wife, surrounded by swamps and tigers and with a crocodile in the pond a few yards from the front door.

Life started to improve for the little English band when Carey and his fellow helper John Thomas were offered the position of managers in a new indigo factory in North Bengal. Mr U. Udney gave them a salary of £250 a year, a third of which Carey put towards running the mission. Unfortunately, the indigo factory was sited on an unhealthy spot, and Carey's son Peter died when only five years old. Dorothy's mental state deteriorated and William himself almost died of a fever.

Carey set about spreading the gospel over an area of 20 square miles. He was able to do this because his time spent working at the factory took up only three months of the year. Sometimes he travelled in a small boat, or sometimes he walked from village to village. Meticulously he wrote down every word he heard spoken in the Bengali language and shortly he began to prepare a dictionary and grammar of that same tongue. A new testament in Bengali was prepared for printing and a printing press was bought from Calcutta for £40. It was on this that Carey printed the Gospel of St Mark.

At 38 years old Carey suddenly found himself without a job, as Mr Udney shut his factory down and returned to England. He was joined by William Ward, the printer, who had come out with Joshua and Hannah Marshman. The Marshmans went on to a Danish settlement, known to the British as Serampore, and Carey decided to join them. They worked together for the next 30 years. This was in 1800, and William was never to return to England. His wife Dorothy died in 1807, after being mentally ill for many years. Carey married three times; his second wife was Lady Rumohr, who was Danish and sadly died in 1821, his third wife outlived him by a few years.

Five families shared the mission and pooled their financial resources. William Carey, one-time cobbler from Northamptonshire, went on to found the Serampore College, and was appointed professor of Sanskrit, Bengali and Marathi at the fort William College at Calcutta. For this he received a salary of £1,500 a year, most of which went on opening up new missions. He held this post from 1801 until 1830. At long last he was recognised as the great scholar, brilliant linguist and translator that he was. William was in his element at Fort William College, and he divided his time between the two seats of learning. At Serampore, which was only 14 miles from Calcutta, he was principal for 24 years and lecturer on Botany and Zoology. It was largely through his efforts in social reform that widow burning and child sacrifice were forbidden. He still preached whenever he could and founded a leper hospital in Calcutta.

The building of Serampore College cost £15,000 and was paid for by Carey and his colleagues, with contributions from private appeals. Carey also started India's first newspaper, called *The Friend of India,* and supervised and translated, with the help of Indian friends, the scriptures into 40 languages, including Chinese. He was the founder of the Agricultural and Horticultural Society of Bengal, and set up 18 missionary stations.

William Carey died on the 9th of June, 1834, aged 73, after 41 unflagging years of missionary work. Humble to the end, his last wish was that his epitaph should be very simple and unpretentious.

At Moulton in West Street, the cottage still stands where he lived and a plaque to his memory is on the wall outside. There is a small but fascinating Carey museum next to his cottage, part of which was the workshop where Carey carried out his shoemaking. It contains the upper panels and reading desk of the missionary's pulpit, his work bench, and the stone trough where he soaked his leather. As well as other mementoes of the great man, there are his church covenant and minute book, and a facsimile of the minutes of the first meeting of the Baptist Society, which took place at Kettering. There is also a first edition of his book *The Enquiry,* and many other documents of the chapel. The museum can only be seen by making a prior appointment. Close by stands the Manse, built in 1955, whilst three years later the William Carey Memorial hall was put up next door. Finally in this attractive row of church buildings, stands the Carey Baptist chapel, where William preached and ministered to his flock, over 200 years ago.

The Legend of Lowick

THE village of Lowick was once deep in the heart of the forest of Rockingham. Even today it is a peaceful place set in a landscape of woods and fields, a few miles from Thrapston. It is an attractive village with a marvellous medieval church and stone cottages, half of which belong to the Drayton estate. The great house is hidden from sight, amidst lovely parkland.

Drayton House has a remarkable history, stretching back to the 14th century. It is a blend of many ages, with its Tudor chimneys, Elizabethan towers and Edwardian battlements. It was built on the site of an early castle, the only part of which remains intact is the massive windowless south wall. Drayton House is extraordinary because over a period of 900 years it has never been sold or let, but has passed from owner to owner by inheritance. Sir Walter de Vere, in the 13th century, assumed the surname of Drayton. It is the grandson of Sir Walter who features in the Legend of Lowick.

One connection with the forest of Rockingham, in Lowick, was the famous Lowick oak. It stood in the grounds of Drayton House until 1968 and was said to

have been a thousand years old. This huge 90ft oak tree had a girth of 25ft. It was probably past this oak tree that young William de Drayton walked when setting out on his hunting trips in the 13th century. The son of Sir Henry de Drayton of Drayton House, he was known to be a persistent poacher of the King's deer in the forest of Rockingham.

The legend records how William arose very early one morning, and called his servants to go with him into the forest. Young William warned his men to be quiet, so as not to arouse his father. He must not know about his son's illicit hunting trips, or else the hated sheriff would fine Sir Henry for William's misdeeds.

'We must tread softly,' said William to his men, 'for it would not do to awake my mother and frighten her. But if she hears us, I think she will guess what's going on, and be glad if we bring back some venison for dinner.' William and his ten followers crept stealthily out from Drayton House, with hounds and bows. His father slept soundly in his chamber but his mother heard him go, and turned herself in bed for luck. 'God shield my son from ill' she murmured, then signed herself and prayed that all might go well with the hunters. A good fat buck would fill the empty larder.

The party came to a clearing in Farming Woods, and William hid behind a tree and waited for the deer to pass by. It was not long before a herd of the beautiful creatures came into the glade to graze. William drew his bow and slew a fat red buck, and then another one. Then suddenly his little footpage came running into the glade, crying out shrilly that he could see the sheriff and his men. They were coming up over the brow of the hill, along the main track through the wood.

The sheriff and his 30 men rode into the clearing on their fine horses. 'William of Drayton,' the sheriff called, 'I know you well. Shame on you, Sir Henry's son, for killing the King's red deer.' William muttered under his breath, 'It would seem that our supper is gone.' Aloud he said, 'The bucks are dead, you can have your lawful prize; the bucks, my bow of Surrey hew and my hounds, for you outnumber us. But before you take away my possessions, I beg leave to blow just once on my bugle horn.'

The sheriff nodded consent impatiently, and William put the bugle to his lips and blew as hard as he could. A tremendous note split the silent glade, where the men waited, wondering at the delay. The sound seemed to rend the very sky apart. Then there came a mighty clap of thunder and the rain came down in torrents.

Frightened out of their wits, many of the sheriff's men fled in terror. Before the stunned gaze of the ten who remained a vivid flash of lightning lit up the darkened wood, and struck the sheriff dead.

As quickly as it had begun the storm was over. Out came the sun and brightened up the dismal glade as though the storm had never taken place.

William and his companions cheered, and young Drayton instructed his men to kneel down in the clearing and thank God for his good grace. Afterwards they picked up the bucks and slung them over their shoulders, and made their way home in a jubilant mood. Everyone ate well at Drayton House that night.

Mutiny!

THE massive ruined summer lodge of Lyveden
New Bield stands in a remote part of the county,
roughly halfway between Oundle and Brigstock. The
building was begun in 1594, but was never finished. It
was designed by Robert Stickell in the shape of a cross.
About a hundred yards from the building is a water
garden, or middle garden as it was originally called.
This immense garden was intended to be an elaborate
creation, with a raised terrace, fish ponds for congers,
and orchards. Sadly it was never developed and nature
was allowed to take over. Though it was extensively
cleared by the National Trust in 1980, it remains a
secret, overgrown place.

The water garden would probably have looked very
much as it does today some 250 years ago, when a
dramatic confrontation took place in this vicinity
between over a hundred Scottish mutineers from the
famous Black Watch regiment and English dragoons.
It was a long and strange journey which brought these
112 deserters from the Highlands of Scotland to the
dense forest of Rockingham in the year of 1743.

The Watch was an independent company of
clansmen, first raised in 1667. When it was
re-established in 1725 by George I, a new tartan was

invented, which was made from the natural dyes of heather and blaeberry. These merged into a dark colour and the regiment became known as 'The Black Watch'. Their uniform consisted of a scarlet tunic, a tartan kilt, a flat round cap with a feather, white stockings and buckled brogues. The men came from a good background, many of them the sons of lairds of farmers, most of them speaking only Gaelic. They were tall, strong men, simple but with high ideals, and considered themselves superior to the English soldier. A lot of them even had their own servants who carried their kit and arms for them on marches. However, Hugh Semphill, the Colonel of the regiment, penny-pinched on the uniforms of his men, reduced their pay and chose poor quality material for their dark plaids. The Highlanders also believed that they had only enlisted to serve in Scotland, and not elsewhere. So it was in this atmosphere of general dissatisfaction that the regiment were told that they were to leave for London to be received by King George II.

Before March was out in 1743, five companies of the Black Watch had set off for the capital in a sullen mood. They were stationed at Barnet and Highgate by the 6th of May. It was about this time that the King decided to leave for Flanders. The proud Highlanders took this as an insult, and their discontent grew.

A crowd of 40,000 people gathered on Finchley common on the King's birthday, Saturday the 14th of May. There was a fairground atmosphere about the event, for never before had nearly 1,000 Highlanders been seen in London. General Wade inspected the

Black Watch and commented in his report that the Highlanders marched well, fired well and were well-built men, but their uniforms were old and worn. Three days later on the 17th of May, a meeting took place on the common at midnight of many of the Highlanders. In the early hours of the morning between 140 and 150 men decided to desert, taking their arms and ammunition with them. Two of the leaders were cousins, Samuel MacPherson and Malcolm MacPherson, son of a laird. The mutineers made good progress and soon reached St Albans, where they asked the toll-gate keeper the way to Northampton.

An hour and a half after they had gone, the keeper reported the strange incident to the Captain of the dragoons. The officer sent a quartermaster after the deserters, to try to persuade them to return. Another rider was sent to the barracks at Northampton and Barnet. Nineteen troops of dragoons from Northampton, Leicester and Huntingdon were sent orders to bring the deserters back to the Tower of London as prisoners. A tough Irishman in his seventies, Brigadier General William Blakeney, was put in charge of the campaign.

The Highlanders travelled by night, hiding in woods by day, intending to march back home. They hadn't molested anyone, the only force they had used was on breaking a door down to take cheese and bacon, which the villagers had refused to give them. The Scotsmen headed for the dense forest of Rockingham in the north of the county, where they knew they would be hard to find. About 40 of the deserters were

39

captured in other places, but over 100 men followed the MacPherson cousins to the thick woods of Northamptonshire.

The Black Watch mutineers came into Lady wood by Sudborough in the early hours of Saturday morning, climbing the ridge of the hill towards Oundle. The thick wood of elm, ash and oak gave them good cover, but it must have been galling for the rearguard of the Highlanders to look down on the Brigstock road, and see the red coated soldiers galloping along the lane beneath them. The deserters now knew that their luck was running out, and soon they must meet up with their hunters.

Perhaps they already had some knowledge of Lyveden, because it would seem unlikely that they would come upon such a good defensive position just by chance. The mutineers made their camp in the wilderness of the water garden. It was an ideal place, surrounded on three sides by water and thickets of trees and undergrowth, whilst at the back of them they were sheltered by Lady wood. In those times this part of the forest came almost up to the walls of Lyveden New Bield.

The men did not light any fires, and slept when they could. They had enough food to last them for a week and 14 rounds of powder each in their pouches. It was decided that they should send a message to the nearest Justice of the Peace. This was Major John Creed, who lived in a grand house called Cobthorne, in West Street, Oundle.

It was dark on Saturday night when Major Creed rode into Lady wood. He could not see the deserters clearly, but they told him plainly that they would surrender on their own terms, and asked him to write to London for a free pardon. John Creed agreed to return as soon as possible with a clerk and went back to Oundle. There he aroused the town clerk to ride to the nearest dragoon officer to tell him that the deserters had been found.

It was not until four in the morning that the Justice of the Peace returned to the wood, with his clerk and writing materials. He was impressed by the Highlanders' bravery and their well placed defensive position. If taken by storm, it would indeed be a bloody battle.

The English dragoons were moving into the area, surrounding the wood at a discreet distance. There were red-coated troopers everywhere in the lanes and meadows about Benefield, Sudborough and Wadenhoe. One can imagine the excitement this military exercise caused in the quiet lives of the local inhabitants.

It was sometime on Whit Sunday that the Highlanders buried one of their men, who had died of exhaustion or illness. A tough member of their party, Farquar Shaw, had also become ill, but he stubbornly stated that he would rather die sword in hand than surrender. It was not until seven o'clock at night that Major Creed sent the reply to the mutineers, refusing the free pardon and 'telling them to give themselves up and return to their duty.'

After debating amongst themselves for many hours, the majority of the Highlanders decided to surrender. In small groups they came out of the water garden and

41

were led to the bivouac of General Blakeney, where they lay down their arms. When the prisoners were counted, it was found that 98 deserters had given themselves up and that 14 men were still missing.

The Black Watch mutineers spent the first night after their surrender in Thrapston churchyard. At two o'clock in the afternoon they were taken to Oundle, and from there to Kettering. At midday on Tuesday they arrived at Northampton. They spent two days in the county town, and from there it took five days to march to the capital. There was tremendous relief in the country when the deserters were caught. It had been imagined that such a large number of 'uncivilized' warriors, roaming the English shires, would play havoc in the countryside.

Farquar Shaw was one of those who refused to surrender. He managed to slip through the network of soldiers guarding the wood and reached Lichfield before he collapsed just outside the town. He was picked up by William Sneyd, who received the usual reward from the War Office, plus 40 shillings extra.

In June, 107 mutineers were tried by court martial. They were all found guilty of mutiny and desertion and sentenced to death. By this time however, public opinion had turned and was now on the side of the Highlanders, who had conducted themselves with dignity. All but three of the men were pardoned on the condition that they were sent to the colonies in America, and never returned to Scotland. Twenty six young and inexperienced men were sent to the garrisons on Gibraltar and Minorca.

The three Highlanders who did not have their death

sentence commuted were Private Farquar Shaw, Corporal Samuel MacPherson and his cousin Corporal Malcolm MacPherson. The prisoners, each wearing a shroud under their kilts, were shot at the Tower of London on the 18th of May, 1743 and buried on the spot.

There is an interesting legend which tells of a grassy mound by the side of Lady wood. This was known by the locals as 'The Soldier's Grave'. It was said that when darkness fell the ghostly form of a Scottish piper, wearing a long dark mantle, could be seen sitting on the mound, playing a mournful tune.

The Extraordinary Village Schoolmaster

I N days gone by it seemed as though every village had
its characters. But surely none were as unusual as
Thomas Carley of Grafton-under-Wood.

This small village lies four miles from Kettering. Its
main feature is the weedy brook which runs down the
main street, crossed by several bridges to the houses
and church. These stand well back on the side of the
road, sheltered by tall trees. A pleasant, unspoilt place,
with stone cottages with thatched or tiled roofs.

It was in this village, that Thomas Carley was born,
in 1754, in an estate cottage belonging to the Duke of
Montagu. His father worked for the Duke. Tragically
the baby was very physically disabled, for not only did
his arms end at the elbows in stumps, but his right leg
was very small, extending only as far as the average
knee, with a tiny foot. His left leg was a normal
well-formed limb. When Thomas was two years old,
the Duchess of Montagu paid his mother Mary a visit.
The good lady was prepared to commiserate with Mrs
Carley over her helpless infant. Instead to her
astonishment when she went into the cottage she
found an active toddler, who was trying to get around

on his disfigured limbs and busily playing with sticks of firewood. Her interest was aroused, for surely this was a child of intelligence and persistent determination. The Duchess promised his mother that she would have him educated and set him up in his own school in the village.

When Thomas was old enough, the Duchess of Montagu sent him away to her husband's estate in Scotland. Whilst he was staying there, he made a carved wooden clock for his benefactress, which kept perfect time. Among his other accomplishments was the ability to write and draw beautifully. He made an accurate drawing of a mariner's compass showing the 32 points of the compass. Underneath in his flowing script he wrote, 'Done in the year of our Lord 1809 by Thomas Carley of Grafton-under-Wood in the county of Northampton, who was born with out hands.' He also made a small printing press about 16 inches square. He cut out the letters himself and operated it by sitting down upon the device.

Thomas was able to perform many of his tasks with the aid of armlets, fixed to the end of his arms, into which were inserted a pen, button hook, knife and any other instruments he required. It is believed that he had rudimentary thumbs at the end of his stunted arms, which enabled him to guide the tools. Carley walked about by using a crutch, which he held under his right arm. He wore a shoe and sock on his tiny right foot, and rested it in a stirrup on the crutch.

In 1777 the Duchess kept her promise and at the age of 23 Thomas Carley was appointed as the first schoolmaster in Grafton-under-Wood. The school was

45

probably a room in a cottage, which would have taken only a small number of boys at the beginning. Thomas also took over the duties of the parish clerk, a post he held for 40 years. Carley was a strict disciplinarian, as was the fashion of those times. The children called him 'Stumpy', and one of his ways of punishing the boys was to make them stand on a brick in the middle of the schoolroom. If the boy set his foot down on the floor, Old Stumpy would crack down on him with his black ruler. Perhaps this was to give the boys a taste of what it felt like to have only one leg to stand on. However, when once he threw the ruler at the wrong boy he apologised and offered him a penny.

Two years before his death Thomas Carley was struck down by a stroke. He recovered enough to rise from his bed, but never regained his power of speech. The parish register records that Thomas Carley of Grafton-under-Wood, born without hands, was buried on the 30th October 1823. His grave is in the churchyard near to the chancel door, but there is no headstone to mark the resting place of this remarkable man who overcame such terrible disabilities.

Thomas Carley was the first member of his family to read and write, but passed his hard-won talents on to his nephew John, who took over his duties as teacher and parish clerk. A small drawing of Thomas Carley hangs in the vestry of Grafton's 700 year old parish church.

The
Culworth Gang

IN the lovely undulating countryside of the
south-west corner of Northamptonshire, seven
miles from Banbury, lies the quiet village of Culworth.
The long attractive street with its houses of contrasting
dark and light bands of stone makes a pleasing picture.

Times were not always so quiet for the inhabitants of
Culworth, for in the latter part of the 18th century a
band of robbers had their headquarters in the village.
Many of the men lived in the parish. At the peak of the
gang's activities the number of men in the
brotherhood was probably 15. This band of thieves
roamed over a wide area of Oxfordshire,
Warwickshire and Northamptonshire. Culworth was a
well chosen centre, for it was remote and had the
advantage of two good escape routes which went
through the village. These were the Welsh road and
the Banbury lane, two ancient drovers' tracks. A
turnpike road through Whittlebury forest carried a lot
of coaches and carts between the county towns of
Oxford and Northampton and this traffic was a great
inducement to highway robbery by the Culworth
Gang. There is a tradition that one of their meeting

47

places and bolt-holes was a barn belonging to Fernhill Farm on the borders of Warwickshire.

The leader of the gang was John Smith, a daring and strong man, whose two sons John Smith junior and William were also members of the association. Other prominent characters in the gang were William Bowers, William Turrell, Thomas Malsbury and John Tack, all labourers from Culworth. Two other important members were Richard Law and William Pettifer. The most flamboyant member was William Abbot who came from the neighbouring village of Sulgrave. To all outward appearances he was a respectable person in the community, being a shoemaker and parish clerk. However, he always carried pistols on him, even when performing his official duties in church.

The gang first came together for the purpose of poaching, which led to more lucrative crimes. They became very successful and planned their exploits in every detail. By some standards their behaviour was not brutal, for they did not maim or kill anyone. The most brutal attack that they carried out was on a Mr Wyatt, a farmer of Sulgrave. In the middle of the night, one of the gang called on the farmer and told him that a drove of pigs needed to be taken in, but as soon as Mr Wyatt went outside, they knocked him down. One assailant jumped on him, bruising him badly about the head and chest. Then they dragged him into the house and shut him and his wife into the pantry. The thieves made off with goods and money to the value of £40.

Only on one occasion do the gang seem to have come

unstuck, when on the 3rd November 1783 they tried to rob the home of Mr Eaglestone. This was 20 miles from Culworth in Old Wolverton in Buckinghamshire, so presumably they had horses to have travelled so far. The gang put on their disguises of smocked frocks and blacked their faces, and seized one of the servants, telling him that they would kill him if he didn't go with them and knock at the door. This he did, and when the door was opened the robbers rushed inside. This time the would-be victims retaliated, as Mr Eaglestone and two of his men attacked them, almost catching the thieves. But in the confusion one of the servants received a terrible blow from one of his comrades, which gave the gang a few precious minutes to get away.

Another crime committed by the gang was on the 18th of January 1785. At about eight o'clock on this dark winter's night, seven of the gang ambushed Mr Richardson, an Oxford carrier. Even though he had his excellent dog with him, this didn't deter them from hitting Mr Richardson on the shoulder with a pitchfork. Then four of them held him and his son, whilst the other three drove the cart behind a hedge and plundered it at their leisure, making off with £140 worth of goods and money. This would seem a trifling amount to us today, but then the daily wage of a labourer was only 5d.

One wonders why the gang were not apprehended for so long, but they seem to have taken meticulous care with their plans. Their friends and neighbours must have had some inkling of their exploits as the men were away so often from home and work. But they were so frightened of the gang that no one would take the first step to inform the authorities.

But time eventually ran out for the Culworth gang. In the end it was two members of the gang, Richard Law and William Pettifer, who became careless and gave the game away. They stopped at an inn in Towcester and because it was late in the evening, they decided to stay for the night. They told Mr Duffin the landlord that they had been to a cock fight at Blakesley. Feeling confident of their safety, they retired to bed, leaving their two bags downstairs. They had told Duffin that they contained a bird in each one. The landlord's curiosity got the better of him and he peeped into one of the bags. To his astonishment he found it contained two smock frocks and masks. Immediately his suspicions were aroused and he sent for the constable. They decided to wait awhile to see what developed.

A few days later there was a burglary at Sewell Farm near Blakesley, adjoining the Banbury lane. The robbers were wearing smocked frocks and black masks. After this Law and Pettifer were arrested, but they denied any knowledge of the crime. As well they might, for it had in fact been committed by another party of the gang, led by William Bowers.

The two suspects, thinking to save their own lives, impeached Bowers and the rest of the fraternity, confessing to 30 other robberies over the previous 15 years. Abbot, the parish clerk, confessed to 17 crimes. After most of the gang were arrested a search was made of their houses, where many stolen goods were found. Some items were found in a secret vault

51

underneath a barn floor, and even in Sulgrave church, hidden there by William Abbot.

In the summer of 1787 a number of the Culworth gang were committed for trial at the Northampton assizes. At the end of the trials five members of the Culworth gang – John Smith senior, Richard Law, William Pettifer, William Bowers and William Abbot were given the death sentence. Abbot was subsequently reprieved and sentenced to be transported to Australia for life. William Smith and William Turrell were discharged through lack of evidence, though why Turrell should have escaped imprisonment is a puzzle, because according to the confession made by Pettifer and Law he had taken part in 21 of the robberies!

The criminal activities of John Smith junior and Thomas Malsbury seem to have gone unnoticed, and it is interesting to note that Malsbury lived on in Culworth for some years until he was involved in an accident with a cart, which knocked him over and killed him on the spot. Jack Tack is said to have absconded when the authorities started to round up the gang.

Whilst awaiting their execution in Northampton gaol, the four convicted members of the Culworth gang spent their time in reading and praying. They accepted their fate with resignation, even William Bowers who at the assizes had been very belligerent, swearing and cursing loudly, and on one occasion jumping up and shouting that 'a man had no more chance there than a cat in Hell without claws.'

John Smith wrote a pathetic letter to his wife, in

which he begs 'of my children to take warning from my unhappy end, that they may turn to the path of virtue, and beg of them to beware of bad company and Sabbath breaking, which is the wish of their dying father.'

It was on ten o'clock on the morning of 4th August 1787, that a mournful procession made its way from the county prison at Northampton along the Kettering road to the gallows ground. Four of the Culworth gang were taking their last journey. The older John Smith, aged 53, and the two much younger men, Law and Pettifer, travelled in one cart, whilst Bowers, aged 36, and two other criminals went in the other tumbril.

On reaching the place of execution, a tremendous crowd of 5,000 awaited them. This was on the corner of the race course, opposite the White Elephant public house. The hangings took place at mid-day, each man being 'launched into eternity', as the euphemism of the time put it, in a similar fashion. A rope was placed around their necks, which was fixed onto a cross beam, as they stood in the cart. Then the signal would be given by a person dropping a hat and the cart would be withdrawn, leaving the man to hang a few feet from the ground.

The execution of the four leaders of the Culworth gang brought about the end of nearly two decades of house thefts and highway robbery around the countryside of Culworth. Never again in that corner of Northamptonshire did a notorious gang of robbers ride out on dark nights to terrorize and victimise innocent citizens.

The Miracle
of the Geese

WEEDON Bec lies close to the Roman Watling
Street, now the busy A5. 'Bec' is derived from the
church's connections with the Abbey of Bec Hellouin
in Normandy as early as the 12th century.

The parish church of St Peter is said by the local
people to be separated from the rest of the village by
fire and water. For the viaduct railway of the main
Euston line was built a few hundred yards from the
front gate (this being the fire part) and at the back of
the church is the high embankment of the Grand
Union Canal. Sandwiched in its damp hollow between
these two giant industrial edifices, the church still
manages to present a pleasing aspect. The warm tones
of the ironstone-built Norman tower almost turn pink
in the evening light.

The interior of the church is surprisingly large and
light, with a well cared for appearance. The many
windows are unusual for they are set with stamped
quarry glass made by James Powell and Sons of White
Friars, London. In 1981 a lovely new stained glass
window was set in a south facing corner of the church,
near to the main door, illustrating the legend of St

Werburgh. The window was designed by Anthony MacCrae, a local artist who lives in Weedon, and was dedicated in 1982. Another connection with the tale is the Victorian weather vane on the church, in the shape of a flying goose.

The legend of St Werburgh and the miracle of the geese goes back to the early days of Christianity. Weedon was the main seat of King Wulfhere of Anglo-Saxon Mercia in the 7th century AD. He was a heathen who married a Christian woman, Ermenilda. Later on in his life he was converted to Christianity, and was the first Mercian king to be baptised. He was said to have helped the abbey at Medeshamstede, now known as Peterborough.

Wulfhere and Ermenilda had four children and his daughter Werburgh was born in Stone, Staffordshire. Even as a young girl Werburgh was interested in the Christian faith and she made a vow to become a nun. Her father was against the idea and refused to give his permission, for he wanted her to marry Werbod, one of his nobles.

Wulfhere died in AD 675 and Werburgh and her mother entered the religious house at Ely. Once there Princess Werburgh changed from the rich clothes of her father's court and dressed in the dark grey habit and simple veil of a nun. Right from the start of her training, Werburgh took on the most menial of tasks with a willing and cheerful attitude.

Ethelred, who succeeded his brother Wulfhere as king, established a convent out of the royal residence at Weedon. He entreated Werburgh to come back to her old home and preside over the convent as abbess.

Werburgh spent much of her time at Weedon Bec and it was here that she performed her most famous miracle. One summer Weedon had been plagued by an immense flock of wild geese who descended on the cornfields in the neighbourhood and gobbled up all the crops. No matter how the farmers and villagers tried to frighten off the birds they wouldn't move and went on eating the corn and fruit. At last the desperate people went to the convent and asked if they could speak with Werburgh. They begged her to help them to get rid of the geese, or else they would starve that winter. The abbess listened to them sympathetically, and told them to go home and all would be well.

Werburgh told her servant Alnoth to go out into the countryside and round up the geese and drive them into pens within the abbey courtyard. Alnoth stared at his mistress in astonishment. 'Drive wild geese into captivity? It is impossible', he said. 'Do as I say', ordered Werburgh, and the mystified servant went and did as she asked. When he went into the fields, he expected the geese to be suspicious of him as he approached. But to Alnoth's amazement they stayed where they were, and when he told them to go to his mistress, the birds walked towards the abbey. Alnoth was able to drive them along the track like tame animals. For not one of them tried to fly away, but they waddled along the path with bowed heads as though ashamed of their bad behaviour.

The huge flock of geese assembled in the courtyard, quietly, as they waited for Werburgh to inspect them. The abbess chastised them for their greed and told them that they would be imprisoned for the night.

They stretched their necks forward as though asking for forgiveness. They hated to be confined like domestic beasts, but they knew they must endure their punishment for one night. During the dark hours of the night, a kitchen servant crept stealthily to the pens and popped a sack over the smallest of the geese, thinking he would have a tasty meal.

In the morning Werburgh came out and told Alnoth to release the geese. Before they departed she addressed them and said that they must never return to Weedon again and devour the crops. The geese started to beat their wings and prepared to fly away. Then it was as though they had looked about and found that one of their company was missing. The din they made was tremendous, no one in the building could hear themselves speak for the honking and the cackling outside in the courtyard. Werburgh went to see what all the noise was about, annoyed to see that the geese had not left. The abbess became calmer as she realized that the geese were distressed, and sensing what was wrong she told Alnoth to investigate the kitchens. He went off and came back with the missing goose, and the culprit who had stolen the bird. Luckily the man had not killed it yet, and Werburgh was able to reunite the bird with his flock. Immediately the geese rose into the air and disappeared from view.

Werburgh continued to live at Weedon, and through her piety and goodness saved many criminals from a life of vice. She lived very frugally and only ate one meal a day. But her life of hardship didn't seem to do her any harm, for she lived to a very old age.

Werburgh died at Trentham in Staffordshire on the

3rd of February AD 699. She was buried at Hanbury, where her corpse remained until AD 708, when it was disinterred and transported to an ornate shrine. This was done in the presence of King Coelred and many bishops, who found the body to be incorrupt. When the Danes invaded the country Werburgh's remains were removed to Chester, where Ethelfleda built a convent for the saint's relics. In the course of time a grand church was built on the spot, which became Chester Cathedral. In the reign of Henry VIII the shrine was broken open and the relics of St Werburgh were lost forever.

St Werburgh became the patron saint of women and children, and strangely enough no wild geese have ever settled on the fields of Weedon Bec since the time of the miracle.

Dionyfia
the Female Knight

CLOPTON lies on the Huntingdon edge of the county, a tiny place. Drive slowly as you approach it, or you might go straight through without realizing that it is a village.

It hasn't got a proper village street, just a few brick-built houses on one side of the road, and a pub called the Red Lion. The church of St Peter was designed in late 13th century style, with a saddle-back tower, and consecrated on the 3rd of July in 1863. The old church was allowed to fall into ruins when the tower was struck by lightning. Nothing now remains of it but part of the churchyard, an eerie place of old tombstones standing in a wood, with trees growing through some of the graves. This ancient graveyard can be found at the back of Clopton Manor.

Clopton Manor stands in extensive grounds on the opposite side of the road from Home Farm. Though the house looks very old in a Gothic way, in fact it only dates back to 1907. It blends very well with the ancient wing of the Tudor mansion and gatehouse tower.

Clopton Manor has a long and fascinating history, mostly connected with the powerful Dudley family,

who married into the estate in the 14th century. But Clopton has a legend which goes back to an even earlier time than the Dudleys.

Walter de Gauntkort was a sly and despicable character. He fell out with most of his neighbours, and particularly offended a young handsome knight by the name of Robert de Hofford. Sir Robert challenged Walter to a duel, and he reluctantly agreed, for like many bullies he was a coward. The day for the duel arrived and he decided to send his lovely daughter Dionyfia to fight in his stead. After all, daughters were expendable. He knew she was a plucky girl, and had sometimes practised with the lance, with her brothers in the courtyard of the manor house.

Dionyfia was only 19, but was bold and adventurous. She was helped into a small suit of armour by her father, who then went and hid. Then her young squire helped her onto the saddle of the great war horse *Bayard* which belonged to her father. The girl carried her hollow shield, her lance strapped to her waist.

The squire led the horse to the field in Clopton village, where all the local people were assembled to watch the thrilling event. Robert de Hofford was already there, waiting impatiently. The knight and Dionyfia faced one another on their horses, a hundred yards apart, and at a signal the two steeds galloped towards one another. The maiden struck Sir Robert on his shoulder with her lance and with a single blow knocked her opponent off his mount. He fell to the ground with a mighty thud. The crowd were astonished, thinking that the youthful knight had been beaten by the much older and unpopular Walter de Gauntkort.

Robert's followers rushed up to him, anxious to see if he had been hurt or, worse still, killed. Unfastening his helmet, they were relieved to see that he was only bruised and winded. His vanquisher was helped down by her squire, and Dionyfia motioned her servant to remove her helmet. To everyone's amazement a mass of golden hair tumbled onto her shoulders. The spectators realized that Sir Walter had tricked Sir Robert by sending his daughter to fight his battle for him. Cheers went up from the crowd, and the girl bent over the fallen knight. 'I hope I didn't hurt you too much,' she said. Robert gazed up at the beautiful face and fell in love at first sight. 'It was worth a tumble,' he said.

The tale has a romantic ending, for Dionyfia married Robert de Hofford. One tradition says that for ever afterwards their family crest bore an illustration of a woman's head wearing a helmet, with hair dishevelled and throat latch unfastened.

It would seem that William, the brother of Dionyfia, inherited some of his father's underhand ways, for before his marriage he cut down a fine grove of ash trees which grew in the churchyard to build a new manor house at Clopton with them.

William married a girl named Ivetta at the place of her birth and as they were coming back along the road to Clopton to take up residence there, they could see in the distance a building in flames. They came closer to the village and saw to their horror that it was their new manor house. When the newly weds arrived they found that the house, together with the provisions which had been prepared for their wedding feast, had been destroyed by the fire. William de Gauntkort took this as a judgement on himself for taking the trees from the churchyard and using them for his own material gains. To make amends he gave a lot of his lands and property away to religious orders and eventually entered a monastery.

The manor house at Clopton has been converted into several private apartments, and the ruined wing of the ancient hall has been restored. But the memory of its past owners and their deeds, heroic and otherwise, lingers on in Clopton.

Kettering's Big Day

IT was an exciting week for Kettering. As one local reporter wrote elatedly, 'for three glorious days Kettering was metaphorically, the hub of the universe and literally the focus of Christendom.' Ten thousand people had visited the town from all parts of Great Britain and different parts of the world, and nearly £10,000 had been raised for the Jubilee fund.

One might well ask, what on earth was this great occasion all about? The time was the first week in June 1842 and the event was the Missionary Society's Golden Jubilee. Every inn and hotel in the town was full, some of the visitors having to stay overnight in the surrounding towns and villages. The main street was choked with a double row of vehicles of every shape and size, from the George Hotel up to the Mission House. Excited groups of people converged on the town, many of them, who hadn't any conveyance, walking into 'The Holy City', as Kettering was called at the time. Flags were displayed by many tradesmen and streamers fluttered in the breeze across the street from the Mission House to the paddock opposite, where an immense tent had been erected.

This marquee was capable of holding 7,000 people and was where most of the services would be held. Although some of the visitors had come on Wednesday, the majority descended on Kettering on the Thursday morning, the 2nd June. The day started off wet and dismal, but the weather soon improved before mid-day. Near the entrance of the great tent, two small tents had been erected, from which were sold volumes issued by the Mission Society and a selection of pamphlets published by the Religious Tract Society. A large portable organ was placed in the marquee, and was played by Mr C. Hillyer, R.A.M., the organist of the Fuller Chapel. The lecture room of the Fuller chapel was opened and used as a reception room and post office between services.

Distinguished Baptist preachers and leaders were present at the Jubilee meetings, but the most popular and admired person present was William Knibb, the famous orator and Baptist missionary and campaigner against slavery. Knibb was born in Kettering in 1803, and was sent by the Society to Jamaica, where he fought for the negro slaves against the tyranny of the sugar planters. His words thrilled the eager congregation when he spoke of their brethren in that far away country. As well as speaking at the great meetings in the tent, Knibb was asked to preach in the chapels to the overflow gatherings. Altogether he was the life and soul of the celebrations and attracted immense crowds whenever he spoke.

The beautiful parish church in Kettering was not left out of the three-day festival, for the building was thrown open to the nonconformists, so that they might look round it, and the rector ordered that the bells should ring out throughout the day in honour of William Carey, the great pastor and Baptist missionary.

To find out more about the roots of the Missionary Society we have to go back to an historic meeting in Widow Wallis's house, on the 2nd October 1792, when 14 young ministers met to form a society 'for propagating the gospel amongst the heathen', which they called The Particular Baptist Society, now known as the Baptist Missionary Society. They agreed to the plan round Mrs Wallis's mahogany table in the small back parlour.

Amongst the pastors present were the Rev Andrew Fuller, who was appointed secretary, and the Rev Reynold Hogg as treasurer.

The 18th century house in which the society held its first meeting was previously lived in by Mr Beeby Wallis, a dyer in the Kettering wool trade. Beeby was a generous benefactor to the Baptist church in the town, where he was a deacon. Mr Wallis and his wife Martha probably moved into the house in 1770. They kept open house for visiting ministers and lay people, which led to the house being called 'Gospel Inn'. After Beeby's death at the age of 57, his widow still continued the hospitality, and when she heard that Andrew Fuller was looking for a suitable place to hold an important meeting Martha willingly offered her home for the venue.

Today this lovely stone-built house is still standing. It has a cement, skimmed frontage painted cream, and now overlooks a busy car park, where once was the paddock on which was erected the monster tent in 1842. In 1909 Mr Stockburn who was then occupying the house, gave permission for a bronze plaque to be fixed to the wall in front of the house, which commemorates the formation of the Missionary Society. In the lower portion of the wall, underneath the plaque are the words,

'Expect great things from God,
Attempt great things for God.'

This couplet summed up the text from Isaiah 54:2 and 3, on which Carey based his sermon at Nottingham, which led to the historic meeting in Mrs Wallis's small parlour.

In 1973 the house was purchased by the Baptist Mens' Movement Housing Association for sheltered accommodation. Eventually the property was turned into eight flats. Further building took place at the rear of the house when the Martha Wallis Court was completed in 1987, comprising 38 flats for elderly residents and two warden's flats, communal lounge and other facilities. The complex is set in attractively landscaped gardens.

It is still possible to see the back parlour where the auspicious meeting took place in the latter part of the 18th century, if one makes an appointment. There are also many interesting photographs and documents about William Carey and the Baptist Missionary Society in the entrance hall of the house. Also in this lobby there is a handsome black fireplace, with tiles with scenes from the Old Testament. It was installed in the house in 1976, after being found in an upstairs room of Timpson's shoeshop in Market Street, Kettering, where the Yorkshire Bank now stands. It came originally from the Mission House but was removed, together with several other fireplaces in the 1920s, when the house was modernised and adapted as a guest house for missionaries on furlough. The Mission House has had (and still has) many visitors from all over the world. One of the most distinguished visitors was General Booth, founder of the Salvation Army, who went to have tea with Mr Stockburn on the 18th of July 1907.

Almost opposite the Mission House is Chesham House, which has an historic past linked with the 'Gospel Inn'. Chesham House, which was built in 1762, was where Thomas Gotch, the shoe manufacturer, lived. Gotch played a leading part in the founding of the Missionary Society, by helping William Carey's work with encouragement and monetary gifts.

Finedon's Haunted School

IN 1712 a charity school for girls was built in Finedon by Sir Gilbert Dolben. It was a solid looking building with a thatched roof, and its purpose was to provide children from poor homes with board and education. They were taught to knit, sew, spin and to make lace. The main employment seems to have been spinning, and the profit from their work was used for the upkeep of the school. In later years the trade of spinning declined and the function of the school was changed. Instead six girls were taken in to be trained for domestic service. The charity supported them entirely whilst at the school, until they were old enough to leave, when a suitable position was found for them. Each girl was given £3 to buy a new outfit on their departure. By 1732 the number of girls had risen to 20.

Nearly a century later, on Christmas Eve in 1823, the girls of Finedon charity school were terrified by strange knocks and bangs all over the house. A violent thumping took place upon the inner doors, as if by a heavy hammer. At the same time the door latches rattled madly up and down. Then the doors flew open,

and if shut by anyone, would burst open again, preceded by a tremendous thump on the middle panel of the door.

The noises carried on into the New Year. At times it seemed as though the whole house shook, especially in the school room, where the beams and rafters gave the impression that they were about to fall down. These disturbances continued incessantly over the next few weeks, until the children were moved away to another house a good distance away in the town. Several people were set to watch the charity school, but nothing more occurred.

But that was not so in the building where the girls were now staying, for similar noises started up again. It was decided that the behaviour of three of the girls was suspicious. Maria Hacksley, Sarah Durbin and Hannah Randall were accused of playing tricks and telling lies. They were expelled from the school on the 5th of February, 1824.

The matter wasn't allowed to rest there though, for the stories of the school being haunted continued to spread. Many scores of people came from miles around to stand outside the school, in the hope of seeing or hearing something of the 'Finedon Ghost', as it became known. As in other sensations of that time, the happening was put to verse, in this case by a Mr Thomas Dexter. It was printed by Whitten of Wellingborough and was sung to the tune of Calder Fair. The first verse went as follows:

Say have you heard the story told,
Now gaining great renown.

71

About the famous haunted house,
That stands in Finedon town,
Where noises loud and dismal
Both day and night abound.
One moment in the upper rooms,
The next upon the ground.

Even though the three young girls had been dismissed
from the school on the grounds that they had caused
the noises by playing tricks, the belief that the school
was still haunted continued. Local people came to
attribute the supernatural occurrences to the special
powers of the Dutch Doll. This curious possession of
the school was a wooden effigy of a charity school girl.
Known in Finedon as the Dutch Doll, it was beautifully
made and painted in the fashion of the Stuart period.
It was about three feet tall, and in the right hand it held
a bible, whilst in the other it held a scroll, on which was
written 'Search the Scriptures'.

In the time of the charity school's headmistress Miss
Kay, from 1863 to 1890, her policy was to punish
naughty children by locking them up in the cellar with
the Dutch Doll. Originally the effigy had been fixed
over the front door of the school, until for some reason
it was taken down and stored in the cellar. One can
imagine what a frightening experience it must have
been for small girls to have been locked in a dark room
with this life-like figure. Small wonder that their
imagination worked overtime, and gave rise to tales of
how the doll walked on its own accord.

The Dutch Doll was eventually moved to the church
and mounted on the west wall, after the closure of the

girls school. Sadly this marvellous wooden doll was stolen from the parish church of Finedon in 1981. The charity school is still standing, but is now a private residence.

The Second Icarus

THE most unusual monument in the county is in a field near to the village of Stanford-on Avon. A public footpath crosses the field near to the classical column, although it is visible from the Stanford to South Kilworth road. The monument was erected in 1907 to the memory of Lieutenant Percy Pilcher, who had a fatal accident on the spot where the column stands, by the Royal Aeronautical Society. The Ionic pillar stands on four rough-hewn steps, which at the base are five yards square. On one side of the base are the words, 'Percy Pilcher, Pioneer of Aviation, fell here in Sept 30, 1899,' and on the other side are two words in Latin 'Icaro Alteri' – to the second Icarus.

Percy Sinclair Pilcher was a man ahead of his times. If fate had been kinder to him, he might well have become the world's first pilot of a powered aircraft. For he had already had ideas on the subject when in 1897 he had taken out a patent for a powered flying machine, based on his experience of balance and control gained from flying a glider.

He had been impressed with the successes of a German aviator, Otto Lilienthal, who flew 100 yards in a glider in 1892. Percy went to visit him in Berlin of that year and was advised by Otto. Two years later he designed and made his first glider, *The Bat,* in which he made the first controlled flight in this country, by taking the glider up a hill near the Clyde and leaping into mid-air. Pilcher studied at London University and then went up to Glasgow to become a lecturer in Naval Architecture and Marine Engineering in 1893. A great scientist of the day, Lord Kelvin, allocated Pilcher a room at the university to carry out some of his experiments on aviation, although he didn't have much faith in them himself. Other gliders followed, *The Beetle, The Gull* and *The Hawk.*

Pilcher and his sister Ella moved to Eynsford in Kent, where he had a small workshop. It was here in 1897 that he made his biggest glider, which was designed to carry a motor. Previously he had paid a visit to America, in the hope of buying a two-horse powered oil engine, and two driving propellers to put under each wing of a new glider he was planning to build. When he failed to find such an engine, he returned home and in 1898 went into partnership with W. G. Wilson, a man who later was to become famous as one of the first designers of the tank. Together they designed the Wilson Pilcher car.

His sister was a staunch supporter of her brother and would often accompany Percy when he went into the countryside to make trial flights. Ella would sometimes run along towing her brother to get him and his machine off the ground. If this failed, Pilcher would use a farmer's horse.

It was at this stage that Percy decided to ask his

friend Adrian Verney-Cave, who was the son and heir of Lord Braye who lived at Stanford Hall, if he could carry out flying experiments on the estate. Although he brought three machines down to Stanford, it was in *The Hawk* that he decided to put on a demonstration for his friend. The site chosen for the show was over the river Avon from the stately home on Northamptonshire soil, for the river divides Leicestershire from this county. Thus the scene was set for the experimental flight which took place on the 30th September, 1899.

Large crowds gathered at Stanford to watch 'a man fly'. They had come from Rugby, Birmingham and from different parts of Northamptonshire. The weather had been bad all day, and it was still drizzling with a gusty wind, when Percy made his third attempt in the afternoon. It was against his better judgment, but he tried because he didn't want to disappoint so many spectators. Two previous attempts had failed because of the line breaking which was attached to his machine.

Then Percy, all dressed in black, stepped into his aircraft, *The Hawk*. He had made the fragile glider himself out of bamboo and piano wire, and covered with Egyptian cotton. The two great wings, which were sodden with rain after being left out all night, had a span of 23 feet and an area of 180 feet. There was a hole so that his head and arms were above the wings. There were no movable parts on the glider, although there was a rudder; control could only be effected by moving the body. The contraption was launched into the air by horses pulling it with ropes and pulleys. He reached a height of 30 ft and a distance of 200 yards and then began to make a gradual descent. The excited crowd ran after him, and then suddenly to their horror a bamboo rod in the tail end snapped and the glider collapsed, turned over and dived 20ft to the ground.

Pilcher's sister Ella, the Hon Adrian Verney-Cave, the Hon Everard Fielding and Doctor Stewart were amongst the first to reach the scene of the accident. Carefully they lifted off the wreckage and removed Percy. They found him unconscious and badly injured, with broken legs and severely concussed. Because he was so seriously injured they sent for his relatives, but sadly Pilcher died at 3 am on Monday morning without regaining consciousness. He was 32 and had made history by being the first man in Britain to fly a heavier than air machine. But at what a cost! The inquest was held at the Hall, where the jury returned a verdict of accidental death, and stated that 'It was regrettable that Mr Pilcher had lost his life in perfecting something, which had it been successful would have brought some good to the world.'

The Barber of Stanwick

STANWICK is very close to Raunds in the north-east of the county. It is famous for its lovely church, which is built on a hill, with its tall spire soaring over the Nene valley.

In the old Duke of Wellington, one of Stanwick's oldest inhabitants can be found every Sunday lunch-time, sitting in his usual corner enjoying his regular pint of Webster's beer. He is Mr Frederick Morris, aged 90, the village barber for many years. Freddy, as he likes to be known, was born on the 21st of November in 1899 in Stanwick. He was the third son of four boys. His father was a bricklayer and was also steward of the working men's club for 13 years.

Freddy is a natural 'tale teller', and just to listen to his yarns is to be transported back to another age. When he was young, the village was smaller, prettier and cleaner. Long avenues of trees, mostly elms and oaks, stretched along all the roads out of Stanwick. The roads were covered in a white dust, for there was no tarmacadam, and if there was a hole in the road it was filled in with flints. Crime was almost unknown and if Freddy or his brothers accidentally broke a window they were scared stiff of the consequences. There was much more respect for older people and their betters. If an older man or woman were coming towards Freddy or his pals, they were expected to step aside to let their seniors pass by. It was also the custom to doff your hat if you met any of the 'toffs'.

At school they had James French as their teacher. He was a strict disciplinarian and was fond of using the cane. When it came to Fridays, Mr French set them a verse of scripture to learn off by heart over the weekend. On Monday mornings, he would pick out one or two of the boys at random, and he expected the pupils to recite the verse off perfectly. Woe betide the boy who couldn't remember it, for Mr French would make him come out in front of the class, where he would be given four whacks of the cane. But Freddy didn't believe that the beatings did them much harm.

He can remember one tale that was passed down to him by his father, about the 'dripping bell'. In the 19th century an influential family lived in the village. They were great entertainers and very often at weekends they had big house parties. The dinners were sumptuous and enormous joints of beef were served to the guests. There was always lots of dripping left over from these immense joints of meat, and the master being a public spirited man, would get his butler to stand at the gates of his property and ring a bell. This was on Monday mornings and anyone in Stanwick who wanted dripping would go up to the great house.

When they arrived at the house, a servant would be there to greet them and fill their various containers with dripping. It was a gesture greatly appreciated by the poor people of Stanwick.

The village had a good band in the early years of this century. They were busy rehearsing for an important contest which was drawing near. Then their best musician, Owen Gates, lost two of his teeth, which made it impossible for him to blow his tenor horn. Rather than let his friends down, Owen got the old village carpenter, Chrissie Clark, to make him a couple of wooden teeth. Mr Gates wore them at the band contest, and Stanwick band gave one of their best performances.

The Great War came and Freddy and his two older brothers joined the army and went out to fight in France. Fortunately they all survived the war and came back home, although William the eldest was gassed and Dennis, the second son, was taken a prisoner of war. Freddy was the lucky one, he only caught a fever.

After the war Freddy found it very hard to get a job. He tried his hand at various occupations, bricklaying, shoework and gardening. Eventually he was offered a position as a trainee barber at Raunds for a wage of a pound a week. In 1927 the barber's shop became vacant in Stanwick, next to the post office. Freddy decided to take over the business at a rent of three shillings a week. At that time shaves were twopence and hair cuts were fourpence. Some of the men in the village could only afford one shave a week. There wasn't much work in the area, mainly farm work and the lime kilns. The first week in his own shop he

81

earned 45 shillings. Freddy has a fund of stories about his experiences as the village barber.

One of his regular customers was Charlie Knight, a groom. Charlie sat down in the chair and the barber started to give him a trim. There were two or three customers in the shop, waiting for their turn. Suddenly Charlie slipped down in the chair and his eyes closed. One of the customers said, 'What's the matter with Charlie?' Freddy replied, 'I don't know, I think he's had a fit or something.' Two of the men lifted Charlie up and laid him out flat on some of the chairs. Someone said, 'Blimey, I think he's gone.' Freddy agreed that it looked like it, and carried on to his next customer, for after all he had a business to run. Charlie wasn't a young man but he had always seemed so fit.

There was a woman in the village called Mrs Liggins, a good-living woman, she was religious and practised what she preached. When anyone was ill or had died, the folk would say, 'fetch Mrs Liggins,' and although she wasn't a nurse, if anyone cut themselves badly, they would go to her for treatment. They called her the village angel, for she would help anyone.

So when Charlie had his funny turn in the barber's shop, they sent for Mrs Liggins. She came and looked at him and pronounced him dead. Freddy told a customer to go to the post office and phone for Dr McKinns. Another person went to fetch the invalid chair to carry Charlie's body away. The wheelchair was kept at Mrs Liggins' house, and if anyone was taken poorly, they put them in the chair.

Then somebody shouted that Charlie had opened

his eyes. They went to look at him and the would-be-corpse asked, 'Where am I?' 'Tell him he's in the barber's shop', said Freddy. A man came in with the wheelchair and tried to persuade Charlie to get into it. He refused point blank. 'I'm not going in that', he said, and someone had to walk him back home. In the meantime the doctor had arrived and wanted to know where the patient had gone. When Freddy said that Charlie had gone home, Dr McKinns was cross and said that they should have kept him in the shop.

Freddy reminisced, 'You wouldn't believe it, but the very day after he'd died in my shop, Charlie Knight was out pushing a barrow of coke to the church.' (In his spare time Charlie used to keep the coke-burning stove going that heated the church.) Fortunately Mr Knight lived for a good number of years after his black-out.

Freddy recalled the time in 1911 when there was a flood in the village. Some of the men were clearing a stream where the rubbish had blocked its passage underneath the road. One of them, Studdy Adams fell backwards into the brook. The fast current swept him underneath the road and he came up the other side. Studdy was thrown up on the bank and was luckily none the worse for wear. Afterwards he was known in Stanwick as Captain Webb, much to his annoyance. He had a brother called Occhey Adams, who used to kill pigs. One day he stuck a pig with his knife and then threw it into a barrel of brine. The poor animal should have been dead, but to his horror it jumped out of the tub and ran down the garden. Occhey ran after the pig and caught it and threw the pig into the brine for a second and final time.

Freddy retired in 1966, aged 66, after being the village barber for 39 years. The charge for haircuts when he finished was three shillings, not much compared with today's prices. He has seen the village change a lot, from a tightly knit community, where the inhabitants made their own amusements, to a far more affluent but casual society. For all that Freddy believes that village life is to be recommended.

Blisworth Tunnel

NORTHAMPTONSHIRE can claim to have one of the longest tunnels in the country. Known as the Blisworth tunnel, it is nearly two miles long.

In 1793, the construction of the Grand Union Canal began. It was a very ambitious scheme, to make a waterway directly from Oxford to London. James Barnes from Banbury was employed to carry out surveys for the route and James Jessop was the engineer for the project.

One of the great difficulties in constructing the tunnel was that a long ridge lay across the path of the canal. Stoke Bruerne lies at the foot of this ridge, and three miles away from the A5 road. This used to be the Roman road of Watling Street, which was the first planned route over the ridge.

A company was formed to create 'The Junction Scheme', and the building of the canal began in 1793. It cost at the finish £90,000, a tremendous amount of money in those days. On the hundred mile stretch between Brentford and Braunston, 3,000 men were employed to work on the canal. By the end of 1796 the waterway had reached Blisworth, and work could begin on the long tunnel.

Jessop and Barnes had planned to cut through the hill on the southern side, near to Stoke Bruerne. But the company could not even begin to construct the tunnel until 1802. First a straight line was chosen, using Bruerne church as a guide, 19 shafts were sunk and at the top a horse gin or winch was erected to remove the rubble and to lower men and materials. The debris was then put on the top of the shafts, and the grass mounds with trees growing on top of them can be seen to this day. The industrious navvies toiled for three years under Blisworth hill, with tallow candles to see by as they dug with shovels and picks, blasting a way through the rock with black powder.

It was necessary to divert the village street at Stoke, from what is now Chapel Lane to a new route over the canal bridge below the top lock. The official opening of the tunnel was on Monday the 25th of March 1805. A distinguished crowd gathered at Blisworth on the day, with Bevan and Telford, the two famous canal engineers amongst them. The first boat through the tunnel was a Paddington packet boat called *The Marquis of Buckingham*. This was early in the morning and it joined the other boats waiting at the Blisworth end of the tunnel to start off the grand procession. The Company Committee, which consisted of Messrs Praed, Mansell, Unwin, Parkinson and Smith, together with other important proprietors and several engineers employed on the canal, then entered onto the boats.

The procession moved off at 11 am accompanied by a band playing and cheers from the spectators. The boats passed into the pitch darkness of the tunnel, which was relieved at intervals by flambeaux and lights. The company were greatly impressed by this superbly built brick archway, which was 18 inches thick, 15 feet wide, 19 feet high, and 3,080 yards in length. The height of the hill above the tunnel being for a good distance, 60 feet. The boats took an hour and ten minutes to go through the tunnel to the south end, where they were met by an applauding throng of 3,000 people. The procession moved on through the seven locks at Stoke Bruerne and on to Stony Stratford.

The principal company retired to the Bull at Stony, and sat down at six o'clock to an excellent dinner, at which there were 120 people, with Mr Praed as the Chairman. Amongst them was that remarkable man Mr Barnes, the contract engineer for the tunnel. Although he could not read or write, he had a brilliant memory and carried all the estimates and calculations in his head. They drank to the health of 'Old Barnes' as he was known. He was asked to make a speech, and Barnes obliged them by saying, 'Mr Chairman and gentlemen, I beg to return you my thanks, and since we are met together, and the tunnel ended, the least said the soonest mended.'

From 1805 the canal had 40 years of prosperity. It is difficult for us to imagine the bustle and activity of the place when there is very little commercial traffic on the waterway today, what boats there are being mostly for the holidaymakers. Living standards in the area improved as goods were brought in cheaply by the boats, especially coal and crockery. When the practice of propelling the traffic through the tunnel with a long pole died out, the method of legging the boats was brought in. Because Blisworth tunnel was so wide, it was not possible for the men to lie on the boats and push against the roof or walls with the feet. Instead a long plank was lashed across the boats by the main beam, with the leggers lying at each end. It was a dangerous practice, often resulting in a boatman falling into the water if the plank turned or the lashing broke. A safer device was sometimes used, when specially made legging boards were mounted on two bolts of the foredeck. If an approaching boat was getting near, these bolts were removed quickly and then reassembled. It took a long time to go through the tunnel. The men would often be choked by the smoke from the fires which burned on the craft.

Until 1871 there was a company of registered leggers working at Blisworth. These workers were issued with brass arm bands, on which their number was stamped. The men from Stoke Bruerne were responsible for the northbound traffic and the men at the Blisworth end of the tunnel looked after the south-bound traffic. The Stoke leggers operated from their hut opposite the Boat inn, and the Blisworth leggers from a hut by the bridge opposite the mill. It was an unpleasant and tedious job, and it took two and a half hours to leg a boat through the tunnel. To entertain leggers and relieve the boredom, the boatmen at the tillers would sing popular songs. These were often plaintive love ballads, passed down through the generations, but never put on paper, so sadly they are probably lost for ever. It was necessary to employ leggers because there was no tow path through Blisworth tunnel. The boats were usually drawn by horses, which were led over Blisworth hill by the boat children.

Eventually steamers took over from horse boats. In 1861 a tragedy took place in the tunnel. A company steamer called *The Bee* was on its return journey from Birmingham to London in September 1861, on a Friday evening between five and six o'clock. They were travelling through Blisworth tunnel at three miles an hour. On board were two engineers, Jones and Gower, also two boatmen named Broadbent and Chambers, who were in control of the steering. The men took it in turns to do the job in each department, each shift lasting several hours. *The Bee* was towing another boat, which was not fitted with a screw propeller.

On this particular evening there were five boats passing through the tunnel, two of them steamers. *The Bee* stopped at 'The Stanks', a place where a number of piles were driven in to make a platform for workmen to stand on as the carried out repair work in the tunnel. Here they took on a young carpenter, William Webb from Stoke Bruerne. They proceeded on their way and soon afterwards met two boats in the tunnel, which were being worked by leggers. They became entangled but after some exertion they broke free. The boat which *The Bee* was towing became unloosed and was left behind. One of the leggers who was on board a boat belonging to a Mr Fellows, said that he had shouted out loudly several times but had got no answer from the steamer.

The man stated that the smoke in the tunnel was so

thick that he could not see either of the boats, or the men on them, nor any lights which were usually carried on the front of the engine room. The first time he became aware of the boats was when he came in contact with the rope by which they were attached. Another steamer was following the two boats being worked by the leggers. This gave rise to even more thick smoke in the tunnel, having fatal consequences for the men aboard *The Bee.*

Webb had only been on the barge for a few minutes when he fell unconscious against John Chambers, who was asleep in his berth. Chambers woke up to hear the carpenter moaning and plunging about, but not able to speak. Broadbent passed out and fell into the water; his body was not recovered until some hours later. Chambers then found that one of the engineers was lying in the stoke hole, insensible, and the other engineer who had tried to rescue his comrade had been overcome by the smoke. The two engineers had been badly burned by the fire and the boiler. Chambers too succumbed to the fumes and when the barge had reached the mouth of the tunnel he fell into the water.

The shock of the cold water revived him and he managed to clamber back onto the boat where he instinctively shut off the steam. The barge then made its way slowly to the lock, where the extent of the accident was revealed. William Webb, the carpenter, who had recently been married, had died, so had Edward Broadbent, who left a widow and eight children. Joseph Jones and William Gower, the two engineers, were seriously burned, and were taken into the Boat inn and attended to by Mr Knott junior of Blisworth and Mr Watkins of Towcester. Fortunately the two men recovered, but were not able to return to work for a long time.

The Buttermilk Hall shaft was opened as a result of this awful accident, to give more ventilation in the tunnel. More shafts were opened in 1881, making the number up to seven. Afterwards, mechanised haulage was put in by the company, which had wire ropes to which the boats could be attached. This device was driven by a steam engine. It was not long before this mechanism was dropped and steam tugs were introduced, which lasted until the 1930s, by which time the craft were propelled by diesel. Legging the boats, however, was still compulsory when the barges were carrying explosives. This procedure was only allowed after the tugs had finished for the night, and naked flames had been extinguished.

The Grand Junction Carrying Company ceased to exist when one of their barges, carrying a dangerous cargo of petrol and gunpowder, blew up in 1874. A claim made against the company of £80,000 crippled the firm, making it go out of business. After this disaster a large part of the trade was taken over by small dealers. But with the coming of the railway, the competition was so stiff that many of the boaters had to leave their homes and live on narrowboats.

To give some idea of the extent of the commercial activity in the early part of the 20th century, it was estimated that in 1908 an average of 170 boats a week passed through the top lock at Stoke Bruerne, the majority of them being narrowboats.

The tunnel was closed for repairs in 1980 and was reopened in 1984. Blisworth tunnel is still the longest navigable tunnel in the country. It is well worth spending a few hours at Stoke Bruerne, where there is a fascinating water-ways museum, which is open throughout the year and covers 200 years of canal history.

The
Stone Cross
of Desborough

DESBOROUGH lies on high land surrounded by lovely rolling countryside, with pockets of old woodlands which were once part of Rockingham forest. Today this small town shows little sign of having an historical past, apart from the 13th century church with its graceful tower, and a handful of fine old houses and inns. But if we dig a little deeper, we realise that beneath its modern aspect lies a long and fascinating history.

A stone cross stands in front of a modern shopping parade, at the corner of Buckwell Close and the High Street, set in a rose garden. Not many people give it a second glance as they hurry past it in their busy everyday lives. Which is a pity because the cross has played an important part in the history of the town.

Until the 1930s the stone cross was a striking feature in the centre of the road at the top of Buckwell Street.

It is a square pillar of ashlar stone, its height nearly 14 feet. At the top there is a large capital which

supports a stone ball. The cross was once used as a mile stone on the turnpike road which went from Market Harborough to Oakley in Bedfordshire, and passed through Desborough. On the north face is cut into the stone, '81 MILES FROM LONDON', on the east face 'TO HARBORO 5', and on the west side 'KETTERING 6'.

The stone cross was much more than just a mile-stone for the inhabitants of Desborough. It was the focal point of many of the activities that went on in the town. The toll gates were near to the cross and were in use from the 1700s until 1878, when they were dismantled and removed. When in use, horse and carts and cattle were charged a toll, but pedestrians could go through without paying. The toll house, which was adjacent, was in use until 1968. After the gates were taken down, the toll house became a painter's shop belonging to Kilbonns. Then it was empty for a while, until Burt Harvey turned it into a very good hardware store.

At the beginning of the 1800s poverty was so bad in Desborough that a large number of people out of the population of 831 were on parish relief. 'Pauper labour' was much sought after by employers, and many of them would only accept pauper labourers. On Monday mornings it was a familiar sight to see men standing in a row by the village cross. They were there to sell their services to the employers. The latter, who were often farmers, would come along and choose their workers, usually the men whom they thought would be the most profitable. The full rate of wages was never paid by the employers, which in any case were very low, the balance being paid out of the rates, at the expense of the ratepayer.

For centuries Desborough was a small, farming community and before the turnpike road was opened in the middle of the 18th century, the village had no main roads at all. A little industry came to the village in the 19th century, in the shape of pillow lace, which employed a large number of women and girls. Then a fresh industry was introduced into the town from Coventry and Leicester, this was silk weaving. At first it was carried on in the homes of the workers, until after a few years some factories were opened for the winding and warping of the silk. Several varieties of weaving took place – velvets, terrys, and plushes for silk hats. The industry employed hundreds of men, women and children. In the decades from 1840 to 1860 gentlemen wore fancy embroidered waistcoats, which were made in large quantities in Desborough.

When the fashion for fancy waistcoats died out, as many as 500 workers were thrown out of work in Desborough. A few years later, the silk trade collapsed completely, leading to great hardship in the town. Many of the large houses opened up soup kitchens to help the starving workers. Times only improved when a Leicester boot company opened up a factory in Desborough in 1868 for riveting boots.

The silk weavers were an intelligent and independent class of worker, who responded to the message of collective effort preached to them by a zealous missionary called John Jarman from Clipston. He came to the town in the 1850s and explained the principles of the Co-operative movement to his audience at the stone cross . A small group of pioneers used to meet at the pillar, many of them silk weavers. From this humble beginning the Desborough Co-operative Society came into being in 1863.

The stone cross was regularly used by the boys of the village as a rallying point, particularly on Guy Fawkes, the 5th of November. They would gather round the cross, in the light of the gas lamps, hands in pockets, and watch as some of their mates would strew gunpowder on the road. A large amount of it could be purchased from a local shop for a penny. The lads would then strike a match and set fire to the gunpowder, which would fizz along the street. Sometimes the youths would write letters or make patterns on the ground with the powder.

In the early 1900s the town band would come and stand around the cross and give concerts, and take a collection for the funds. In 1904 the collection for Desborough band was one pound and ten shillings.

During the First World War when food was very difficult to obtain, the residents of the town looked anywhere to get items to supplement their diet. They went blackberrying, mushrooming, gleaning in the fields for corn, and in the autumn months they would go into the woods close to Desborough to collect nuts. If it was a good season for nuts, men, women and children would come back with their pockets and bags bulging. Many of the men and boys would meet at the cross, talking, cracking and eating the nuts they had gathered. The road would be littered with nutshells every night until all the nuts had gone.

On the Feast of St Giles, which is held on the first

Sunday after the 13th of September, relatives and friends of families living in Desborough would come in for the day from out-lying villages, to take part in the celebrations which were held around the old cross.

The stone cross was a meeting place every night for the policemen in the 1920s. The sergeant would be waiting for the three constables, who would arrive on their bicycles, and he would then direct them where to go on their next beat.

The 1920s was the last decade when the stone cross was used by the people of Desborough as a meeting place for their various activities. The 20th century had caught up, and the increasing traffic meant that the cross was no longer a safe place to meet.

It was decided in 1939 to remove the cross to its present position, as the pillar was considered to be a danger to the ever-increasing traffic, and pedestrians as well. At that time Buckwell Street was used by the A6 south-bound traffic which was diverted down High Street and Lower Street, whilst north-bound traffic was diverted up Buckwell Street, where it turned left into the High Street at the top.

The old cross, which had stood there for 200 years, was dismantled stone by stone and re-erected by the side of the road. The bricklayer who carried out the job for Tailby and Sons was Billy Austen from Rothwell. Billy buried data and information inside the pillar, which is still there to this day. Old property at the corner of Buckwell Street was demolished, and a traffic island with a keep-left sign was put in the place of the cross. But at least the cross has been saved for posterity and future generations will be able to stop beside it and ponder, 'Of what was its use?'

Rowell Fair

ROTHWELL, a small town between Kettering and Market Harborough, has retained a lot of its character and some interesting old buildings, such as the Market House, built by Sir Thomas Tresham in Elizabethan times. Nearby stands the Jesus Hospital, founded in the early 17th century by Owen Ragsdale. Probably the oldest and most impressive building in the town is the ancient parish church of Holy Trinity, the longest church in the county. But the town of Rothwell is famous for its Rowell Fair, as well as its architecture.

The fair, said to be one of the oldest annual street fairs in the country, dates back to 1204. King John granted the town of Rothwell a charter to hold it 'at the feast of Holy Trinity for and during five days, that is to say on the Eve of Holy Trinity and on that day and on the following three days.' It is a movable date, being eight weeks after Easter, and Holy Trinity is the Sunday after Whitsuntide. The fair is becoming more popular each year and when Proclamation Day falls on Spring Bank Holiday, the crowds are immense.

On the morning of Proclamation Day the narrow streets of Rothwell are crowded with people. By 5.30 am everyone is making for the parish church on

Squire's Hill, where at 6.00 am the Fair Proclamation is to be read out by the bailiff to the lord of the manor of Rothwell.

A large funfair is set down in Bridge Street and the Market Square. Stalls will be selling all manner of goodies, and traditional fare of lemon cheese tarts and fair hams will be sold all over the town, washed down by hot toddies. The pubs are already open, and will stay that way until night-time. Lucky early risers can partake of appetizing English breakfasts, being served at some of these establishments. At this hour the roads are closed to traffic until the Fair Proclamation has been read out, but afterwards it is a nightmare to drive through the town, especially as the main A6 road goes through Rothwell. These days, the fair is a sedate, controlled family affair, compared with days gone by. Perhaps this is not a bad thing, for in the past the crowds got out of hand, with fights and shop windows being broken.

At one time great preparations were made for the fair. The old men who lived at Jesus Hospital were measured for their new blue coats and breeches. Householders would lime-wash their kitchens, cellars, barns and outhouses. The local farmers would kill their pigs, butchers would slaughter the oxen, and dressers would prepare the tripe. Ostlers, who fixed a wisp of hay over their gateways or stable doors, would have the privilege of taking in, on their own account, the farmers' horses.

Housewives used to try and get their spring cleaning done by the time the fair came round. They could then greet their relatives and friends with a clean house, as many would return to their native town for Rowell Fair. Rothwell was and still is called 'Rowell' by its inhabitants.

Originally the fair was held for the business of selling horses, cattle, sheep, and many goods and articles. The sale of cattle and horses died out before the Second World War, but in the *Kettering Advertiser* of 4th June 1926, an article entitled 'Up in the morning early' describes how 'The cattle – not more than a dozen in all – were stationed near the war memorial where poles had been erected to which they had been haltered. The sale was not very brisk. The horses which numbered about a hundred, were stationed in Fox Street. Amongst the stock, were a number of ponies, for which a good trade was anticipated.' At one time a field off the Kettering road was used for the horse fair.

Now the market has died out and only the funfair remains. The street fair used to commence on Saturday and lasted for the following week, but so much drunkenness and reckless behaviour took place at the fair on Sunday, that the reading of the charter was changed to a Monday morning. One reason for this rowdiness was because of the unrestricted practice of selling liquor from any dwelling which had a branch of a tree, or bush, over its door. These were called 'Bower Houses' which were allowed to sell drinks day and night from Proclamation Day until the end of the week.

The throng of about 2,000 people wait expectantly outside the brown ironstone church for Mr Norman Hall the Bailiff to appear. He is followed by his escort

101

of Halberdiers and they have started off from Wales Street. The nine men represent each reign since James I and each man carries a pike or halberd, with the initials of each monarch on the blade. The crowd goes quiet, after the church clock has struck six times, and Mr Hall reads out the time-honoured words of the Proclamation. Norman Hall is the third generation of his family to be the Bailiff, for his grandfather Joseph Hall was verger of the parish church, which carried the position of Bailiff as well. Norman's father, Reg Hall, followed on with the tradition.

With the concluding words, Mr Hall raises his hat and three rousing cheers are given for the Queen. The vicar's wife gives the Bailiff a traditional drink of rum and milk, and the band plays the National anthem. The procession moves on to the war memorial where the band plays a hymn. Then they all move off to the spot where the New Inn used to be, to the strains of the band playing a march. Though the New Inn ceased to trade as pub some 40 odd years ago, and has since been pulled down, tradition must be observed, and the Bailiff reads out the Proclamation once more. When he has finished speaking the band plays *God save the Queen*. The Obstructionists (often young men of the town) try to stop the Proclamation from being read out at each of the town's pubs. Some of the youths try to grab the pikes off the Halberdiers, a lot of pushing and shoving ensues, and a few mild struggles take place but mostly of a good natured sort. It used to be a very boisterous affair for the strong young men of the town. They would often link arms across the road, to hold up the progress of the Bailiff and his followers as long as possible. Why this custom of the Obstructionists takes place, no one really knows, unless it dates back to the time of that very unpopular sovereign King John, who originally granted the fair charter.

Eventually the procession visits every pub in the town. For the last time the Proclamation is read out by the Bailiff, the participants have their traditional drinks and the picturesque ceremony is over for another year. Most of the sightseers go home for their breakfasts and face another day at work. But those who are fortunate to have a holiday are free to sample the fun of the fair and the hospitality of the public houses!

The World's End

WHAT'S in a name? A lot it would seem when it comes to the old coaching inn, the World's End on the A4500. This establishment with the intriguing name stands on the old toll road between Wellingborough and Northampton in the pretty village of Ecton.

The World's End was not always called by that name. In the 17th century it was known as the 'Globe', and was first mentioned in 1678. It was in the middle of the 18th century that the ancient hostelry was rebuilt with extensive barns and stables along the main road. The original front is now at the back, as the main road used to go by on the south side of the inn, and not on the north as it does today.

There are various stories concerning its strange name. One tradition says that an adjoining paddock was used as a compound for Royalist prisoners, who had been captured at the battle of Naseby in 1645. They were herded into the paddock by the victorious Roundheads, before being marched to London to face trial. Sadly many of the wounded Royalists died there, and for them it became 'The World's End'.

Another local tale tells of how William Hogarth, the famous 18th century artist, painted a new inn sign for the landlord of the Globe, and renamed the hostelry, the World's End. Hogarth is said to have painted the sign, which was a globe bursting into flames, as a tribute to the skills of the landlord, who was renowned for his brewing. The artist took the new name from the paddock which adjoined the property, with its grim associations with the Civil War. On old maps and tithe books the inn was shown as standing on a large triangular piece of land 'entitled The World's End.'

William Hogarth often stayed in Ecton, at either the Globe or the rectory, where he painted a splendid portrait of his friend John Palmer. The landlord of the inn was very proud of the sign that Hogarth had painted for him, which was placed on the opposite side of the road on the greensward. Every night he would take it inside, until one night he forgot to do so and it was stolen, never to be seen again.

The World's End was often the centre of activities in Ecton. In 1759 the inquiry into the enclosure of common land was held at the inn. Hiring fairs were held regularly in the paddock belonging to the old hostelry, where farm workers and servants who wished to change their jobs came to meet their new employers. Ecton Feast was held there, and the field would be full of stalls and all the trappings of the funfair. In the past the landlord of the World's End was a part-time farmer, like many other inn-keepers of the period.

One more legend is attached to the inn, which is said to relate to the Eve of Halloween, on the 31st of

October. At the crossroads which is just past the World's End, a nun is said to appear in the middle of the road at midnight. She holds up her hand and stops any person or traffic from going straight ahead.

In the 18th century a stage coach was travelling fast along the road from Northampton to Wellingborough. It was just before midnight of Halloween and the horse-drawn vehicle had passed the World's End when the coachman saw what he thought to be the figure of a nun standing in the middle of the track. It was imperative that he should reach Wellingborough that night, and he was determined that nothing would prevent him from reaching his destination.

Cursing under his breath for the delay the driver only just managed to bring the coach to a halt within a few feet of the figure. He shouted down to the hooded woman, 'What on earth are you doing here at this time of night? Do you want a lift?' But she never answered. The man got down off the coach and told the nun to get out of the way. But he nearly fainted with horror when he took a closer look at the woman. For underneath the hood where the face should have been, was a ghastly grinning skull.

Trembling with fear he scrambled back onto the coach and tried to force the horses on their way. They refused to budge. They whinnied and shied but would not go past the menacing figure. No matter how hard their master hit them with the whip, the animals wouldn't go any further. There was only one thing to do, the coach must be turned around. With great difficulty, the coachman managed to swing the vehicle

107

and horses around in the crossroads. Then taking the Sywell road, which eventually went to Wellingborough, although by a much longer route, the driver was able to reach his destination after all.

The World's End has recently been superbly renovated and enlarged, but still manages to retain an old world charm. It is well worth a visit, but perhaps not on the night of Halloween!

The
Livingstone Connection

THE Church of St Nicholas in the village of Twywell holds some fascinating reminders of the famous African missionary and explorer Dr Livingstone.

Horace Waller was appointed rector of Twywell in 1874. He was one of the first members of the Universities Mission to Central Africa and one of the chief objectives in his life was to see the end of slavery. Mr Waller was involved in setting up a declaration in Zanzibar which made slavery illegal in that island. He was also a friend of Livingstone and was with him for a time in Africa.

David Livingstone died in Africa on May Day in 1873, and Susi, his native boy, decided that the Doctor's body should be taken back to England to be buried in the land of the 'White Queen'.

Susi and another man, Chuma, were David Livingstone's only friends in his last years, and they carried him on his journeys when he was too ill and exhausted to walk. Their courage and fortitude was phenomenal. They carried him over swamps, through forests and across rivers, and built a hut for him when he was dying. When they realized that Livingstone was dead, they embalmed his body and buried his heart at a place called Chitambo. The loyal servants wrapped his corpse in bark and carried it 800 miles until they came to the sea shore. The body was carried on a pole and at one time they disguised it in a bale of cotton to enable them to pass through a certain tribal chief's country, who would not give permission to take a dead body over his land. Susi and Chuma also accompanied his body on the last stage of the journey to England, where David Livingstone was finally laid to rest in Westminster Abbey in 1874.

After the funeral Susi and Chuma came to live at the rectory in Twywell for a time, where they helped the Rev Waller to work on the diaries of Dr Livingstone. The rector had received a letter from the Doctor asking him to deal with his notes, should anything happen to him. The two natives proved invaluable to Horace Waller, with their knowledge of Africa and the missionary's life. Susi was a remarkable man, servant and friend to Livingstone. It was he who sowed the seeds that the explorer gathered, and cared for them until they got them back to Kew Gardens. In all the years that he was with Dr Livingstone he never lost a scrap of paper, and when the diaries finally arrived at Twywell rectory, not a single entry was missing.

In a glass case in the church are pieces of the actual bark in which David Livingstone's body was wrapped and carried. Other momentoes of the slave trade are preserved here, such as the neck shackles which held the natives as they were marched to the market at Zanzibar, and the pincers which cut the shackles off the prisoners. Another connection with Africa are the beautifully carved oak choir stalls. They are dedicated to the Rev Horace Waller and illustrate jungle scenes alive with animals, including an elephant, a lion and a hippopotamus. Other carvings portray African slaves chained together as they toil through difficult terrain towards the cross, and on reaching it they find that the fetters drop from them. The Rev Waller is depicted on the carvings facing the cross with the slaves.

There is a tradition in Twywell that one of the native boys went back to Africa, and the other one stayed in England. The African who stayed in this country married a French girl, who had two sons by him and one of them married a Twywell girl, so the story made a full circle.

Murder at
Wood Burcote Lodge

ON a peaceful Sunday in November, an elderly
farmer and his family were spending their
Sabbath in a traditional way at Wood Burcote Lodge
near to Towcester.

It was the 30th of November 1873, Advent Sunday,
when John Cox Newitt settled down in his favourite
chair in the parlour. He was anticipating an hour or
more to himself to read the Bible, as was his custom
each day. A flickering candle on the table at his side
was his only light. His wife and son had left in the horse
and trap for evensong at Towcester. A special
missionary preacher was taking the service and they
were very keen to hear him talk on his experiences.
The younger members of the family were away for the
day visiting relatives.

John Cox Newitt had been born 72 years previously
at Bradden, a few miles away. He was the second son of
William and Sarah Newitt. Both John and his brother
William became farmers like their father. At the late
age of 43 John married Mary Brooks at Chasleton
church near to Morton-in-the-Marsh. In 1868 they

moved into Wood Burcote Lodge with their eight children.

As John Newitt peered at the small print in his Bible, reading the lesson for the day, and probably dozing a little, he was roused out of his reverie by a loud commotion coming from the kitchen. Getting up stiffly from his chair he went to investigate.

Harriet Stevens, the young maid, had sat down by the kitchen fire after completing her chores, and started to write a letter. Then she heard someone come into the room. Thinking that it was her mistress and young master, Harriet got up to start to prepare the supper. She turned round and was startled to see a man standing in front of her.

The young servant girl recognised him as a local man, Thomas Chamberlain, who lived one and a half miles away at Lord's Field toll bar on the Whittlebury road. Chamberlain was aged 41 and keeper of the toll gate, and a cobbler by trade. Harriet knew him quite well, having visited his wife and two children several times. She was just about to ask him what he wanted when, without any apparent provocation, the keeper attacked her with a sharp sword that he was carrying. She managed to dodge out of the way, but not without losing some tresses of her hair!

It was at this point that old John Newitt appeared in the doorway. He was carrying his Bible and tried to defend the girl, but Chamberlain turned on him, swinging his sword at him savagely. The maid, screaming, ran from the kitchen to fetch help.

By the time the farmworkers came, it was too late to save him. His mutilated body was lying on the kitchen

113

floor and Chamberlain had fled. One of the men set off to Towcester to get the police. They were quickly on the scene and later went to Chamberlain's home, where they arrested him. The toll bar keeper denied having any knowledge of the murder, although blood-stained clothing was found and at daylight blood-stained footprints were discovered leading to Chamberlain's cottage.

An inquest was held the next day at Towcester in the Pomfret Arms, now called the Saracen's Head. The Newitt family's solicitor was Mr William Whitton and one of the members of the coroner's jury was Mr William Jenkinson, both of whom had very respectable reputations in the locality. News of the murder travelled fast, and because the Newitt family were well liked and well known in the district, tempers were roused. Crowds started to gather in Towcester after the arrest of Chamberlain, and there were growing fears for his safety. On the Monday afternoon a search was made for the murder weapon. The pond in Lord's field was dredged and a heavy cavalry sword was found. This was later identified by an ironmonger in Daventry, who said he remembered selling it to Chamberlain four years previously.

It was on Tuesday morning that Chamberlain was brought before the Magistrates at Towcester, who were Lord Charles Fitzroy and the Honourable Colonel Douglas-Pennant. Chamberlain was committed for trial the same day and sent to Northampton jail. At first it had been intended to take him to Northampton by train, but because of the many threats by the public on his life, this plan had to be changed. Large crowds were already waiting at Towcester, Blisworth and Northampton railway stations. At nine o'clock that night Chamberlain was put into a coach with an armed guard and taken to Northampton by road.

The Lent Assizes were held at Northampton in early March 1874, where Thomas Chamberlain was tried for the murder of John Cox Newitt. Harriet Stevens, the maid, was the chief witness. Since Chamberlain had been arrested, she had received threatening letters and was a very frightened girl as a result. At the end of the court proceedings, the judge commended her bravery. Sentencing Chamberlain to death, Brett warned the prisoner that there was no hope of a reprieve, and the Royal Prerogative would not be sought. Chamberlain was remarkably reticent and seemed unconcerned about the murder and his death sentence.

Some of Chamberlain's friends were esteemed Baptists, which led the Rev John T. Brown of College Street, Northampton to visit him in jail, but Chamberlain repulsed him rudely. When his wife and two children, a boy aged 15 and a girl of eight, and his brother called to make their last farewells, the prisoner made no reference to the dreadful fate awaiting him. During the 20 minute interview the conversation was mostly of a frivolous nature. Chamberlain made only one remark about religion, when he said that 'Even at the eleventh hour, it would take a good many parsons to change him.' The only show of emotion was at the moment his family left the cell. This last meeting took place on the Friday afternoon of the 27th of March.

It was discovered later that Thomas Chamberlain had hoarded a considerable amount of news cuttings on crimes, murders, suicides and burglaries. He had evidently taken a great interest in criminal history. It was even suggested in some quarters that in the absence of a clear motive, this excessive study of crime was the cause of Chamberlain murdering John Newitt. The Newitt family thought otherwise. One of them had seen Chamberlain at Northampton cattle market, the day before the murder. Old John Newitt had made a lot of money from the sale of his animals, and it was more than likely that Chamberlain knew this fact and hoped to steal the cash, not realizing that Mr Newitt had banked it at Towcester on his way home. The toll gate keeper had probably expected to find all the family including the maid, away at church in the evening. It was often the case in the country in those days that people would go out and leave the door unlocked. Chamberlain knew the layout of the farm as he had worked for old John Newitt at harvest times.

Thomas Chamberlain was hanged on the Monday morning of the 30th of March 1874. Rarely can a murderer have met his end with such nonchalance. He even joked with the executioner, whose name was Marwood and came from Lincolnshire. When he reminded Chamberlain at 6.15 am that 'time was getting short', he replied that 'he had never felt better in his life'. As he was being tied up he remarked to Marwood that 'he was strapping him up pretty tight.'

John Cox Newitt was buried in Bradden churchyard on the 5th of December 1873. A simple inscription on his headstone states 'Thy Will Be Done.' This stone can be found on the north side of the church. On the following Sunday memorial services were held at Bradden, Towcester and Whittlebury Church.

The great grand-daughter of John Cox Newitt lives in Northamptonshire and has some keepsakes of the tragic event. The bible with its blood-stained and slashed back pages, which old John was reading on the night he was murdered, his chair and the candlestick, have been passed down and are now in her possession. A poignant reminder of a violent episode in her family's history.

John Clare
Nature Poet

IN 1861 an article appeared in the *Northampton Mercury*, written by John Plummer, a Kettering poet. He described a visit to the county lunatic asylum, where he had gone to see John Clare, Northamptonshire's peasant poet.

Poor, tragic John Clare spent the last 25 years of his life in Northampton's General Lunatic Asylum. It was a grand new building, erected in 1836, and as a hospital for the mentally ill it was a very advanced, humane hospital for the day. It is now known as St Andrew's Hospital.

To understand how such a great and happy poet as Clare, thought by some to be the greatest nature poet that this country has ever produced, should come to spend the last long years of his life in a mental institution, we have to go back to his earliest beginnings in his native village of Helpston, where he was born in 1793. This is a small place near to Peterborough. At one time it was in Northamptonshire, but when the county borders were moved in 1974, it became part of Cambridgeshire.

It is difficult for us to imagine how the countryside

looked in Clare's time. One could see the fens stretching out in the distance for 30 miles, only broken by the towers of Burghley House. The tiny isolated village of Helpston at that time consisted of two streets meeting at right angles, marked with an ancient cross. The church stood nearby and Clare's cottage was further down the high street.

Parker Clare, John's father, was very popular at feasts for his ballad singing and fiddle playing. When he was old enough to earn his living, he became a shepherd. It was whilst tending his sheep on Helpston Heath that he met his future wife, Ann Stimsom from Castor, who sometimes looked after her father's cattle on the heath. They married and lived in part of a cottage in Helpston. In 1793, Ann gave birth to twins, a boy and a girl. The girl was strong but the boy was weak, yet strangely the girl died in infancy, and the boy, John Clare, survived.

At that time the village was surrounded by undrained fens, which were stagnant and covered with mists for a large part of the year. This made Helpston a very unhealthy place to live in for the villagers. The countryside was still not enclosed and little John loved to wander about the open fens, studying in detail the insects and flowers and watching the birds. When the land was finally enclosed it caused John a lot of heartache, for it stopped him from wandering across many of the fields and commons. In his adult life he was to write about the subject in his poems.

John Clare's family were abjectly poor, their daily diet often consisted of only potatoes and water porridge. They were lucky if they got a small piece of wheaten bread, and a small piece of pork on Sundays. His father became crippled with rheumatism and had to apply for parish relief, and remained more or less a pauper for life.

By a tremendous effort on the part of his mother to get sufficient money together, John was able to get three months schooling out of every year until he was twelve. It was whilst at school that he met Mary Joyce, a lovely daughter of a wealthy farmer. With her chestnut hair and blue eyes, she was John's first love.

A stroke of luck came his way when the owner of the Bluebell Inn, next door to his home, offered him a job for a year. It was as groom and gardener at the inn, and the kind landlord said he could have some time each week to continue with his studies. This was a happy time for John, for he wandered about the countryside for hours, after completing his light duties. About this time John started to write ghost stories. The ordinary labourers in Helpston thought he was strange because of his habit of talking to himself, and reading even when he was tending to the cattle.

One of his chores was to go to the mill at Maxey each week to fetch flour for his master. Mary Joyce came into his life again, when he saw her sitting on a stile on his way to the mill. They met frequently over the next few months. Mary was fascinated by the entertaining stories told to her by the pale boy. But when her father found out that they were meeting, he forbade his daughter to see John any more. After all, Clare was very poor and far beneath Mary in the social scale. They never met again and Mary died a spinster. John never forgot her and idolized Mary for the rest of his life, writing many fine love poems about her.

By the time he was 21, he was writing up to six poems a day, often sitting in the fields and scribbling down his thoughts on any scrap of paper that come his way. John wrote about the countryside that he knew, the birds, flowers, the village scenes, customs, folklore and the poverty of the ordinary people.

John started to put some of his best poems together. For this purpose he bought a strongly bound book of blank pages from Mr J. B. Henson of Market Deeping. The curious printer, on finding out why a poor labourer like Clare should want such a book, was amazed to find that the poems were good. He then offered to print 300 copies of a volume of Clare's poems, by the subscription method. John would have to write the prospectus and when enough orders came in, Henson would go ahead and print the book.

Clare was now spurred on to get a better job, and found one at Bridge Casterton as a lime burner. He stayed in a lodging house as his work was seven miles from Helpston. It was a long tiring day of 13 hours but the pay was good. It was whilst at this job that he met his future wife, Martha Turner, as she was walking across the fields. Martha, or Patty, as John always called her, was a milkmaid and was born in 1799. She was a tall, slender, fair-haired girl of 18, with a good natured disposition, and always had a sincere love for John.

Things weren't going well with John's book of poems, as not enough subscribers had been found. Then Clare had another stroke of luck when Edward

Drury, who owned a book shop in Stamford, got to hear about Clare. Mr Drury offered to print John a book of his poems, without having to find any subscribers. He sent the manuscripts to his cousin, John Taylor of Fleet Street, London, who was a publisher. Mr Taylor was impressed by the work and thought that John would be a great poet, because his poetry had a fresh and unusual style.

His first book of poems was called *Poems Descriptive of Rural Life and Scenery*, by John Clare, Northampton-shire peasant, and was published in 1820. John Taylor edited the poems and wrote a long introduction in the first book, and a glossary of the dialect words. The book was successful beyond Clare's wildest dreams. The first edition of 1,000 copies sold out very quickly, then a second edition was printed, and then a third. The critics were enthusiastic about this new poet. The Marquis of Exeter asked Clare to call at Burghley House, where John had once worked as a gardener. He offered Clare 15 guineas a year for life, and John thought his days of poverty were over. Lord Milton, also a local landowner in the district of Helpston sent for John and bought ten copies of his book. Clare left after the interview with £17 in his pocket, the most money he had ever had.

It was decided by his publishers Taylor and Hessey that John should visit London after his first book of poems had been published. He met Lord Radstock, one of his patrons, and Mrs Eliza Emmerson. This lady was to befriend Clare and his family for the next 20 years. He had his portrait painted by William Hinton, but in spite of these exciting events, John was homesick for Helpston.

For all his success as a poet, Clare was still working in the fields, and his fellow workers resented him or laughed at him behind his back. Poor John Clare for all his genius was always hard up, and never received any large sums of money for his books. He was flattered and petted by the public, and was to meet many famous writers of the day, but he suffered from the fact that the public, instead of recognising his talent for what it was, treated him as a bit of a freak, a literate peasant, and his popularity soon died away.

John went on to write two more books of poetry, *The Village Minstrel*, published in 1821 and *The Shepherd's Calendar* in 1827. The sales for both these books were disappointing, after the tremendous success of the first book.

John and Patty had eight children and four of them sadly died before their father. It was in 1830 that John started to show the first signs of his mental instability. Another great change took place in his life, when he and his family moved into a fine, newly built house at Northborough, three miles from Helpston. This was specially built for John by Lord Milton. It had two acres of land and an orchard, and was let to him for £15 per year. This should have been a settled, happy time for Clare. His wife was to run the property as a small holding, and he was to have time to devote himself to writing poetry. But this magnificent gesture on the part of Lord Milton had come too late for John. His mind was exhausted.

In 1835 another volume of his poems was published, called *The Rural Muse*, his last book to be published in his lifetime. Although it was well received, the book did not sell well, which was a bitter diappointment to Clare. His behaviour became more unbalanced, and he became very excitable at times. He was committed to Northampton asylum on the 29th December 1841.

In the spring of 1863 Clare had several apoplectic fits and was confined to bed. He died quietly on the 20th March 1864, aged 70. His body was taken back to Helpston by train. John was buried in the churchyard of his native village, next to his parents.

Though the modern village of Helpston has changed out of all recognition since Clare's day, there are some landmarks which John would have known. The house where he was born is still there, and the butter cross on its circular steps is still next to the old church. Near to the cross stands a fine memorial to John Clare, which was erected in 1869 with funds provided by the Fitzwilliam family and public subscription. The site where it is placed used to be the village pond. His gravestone is on the south side of St Botolph's church; a simple slab with a pitch – pointed shape which bears the inscription, 'To the memory of John Clare. Poets are born not made.'

The children of the village still remember their great poet, for on the anniversary of his birthday, 13th July, they put cushions of wild flowers around his grave. John used to speak of a very old custom in his youth when the villagers of Helpston would take a piece of greensward, full of field flowers, and place it in their cottages as an ornament in the summer. They called them Mid-summer Cushions, a title John had wanted for his last poetry book. Clare would have been touched by the gentle and kindly gesture by the modern children of his native village.